Everyday Practical Leadership

If you want to go fast, do it yourself.

If you want to go far,

Attract

Inspire

Retain

the right people

Everyday Practical Leadership helps you define your YES!

Enable your WHY and show up well!

By **Robert Freese**
Opportunity Group, Inc. – Turning Opportunity into Reality!

Bridge the gap between strategy and tactics, build teams that:

…create genuine Stakeholder value & results

…are proud of their work

… engage in continuous learning

… employ creative win / win collaboration

… provide positive peer pressure and support

… drive accountability across the entire team

… enjoy a feeling of accomplishment & have fun

… retain the best players and grow learners

The leader's end game;
**Attract, inspire and retain the right people to build
win/win/win for your Stakeholder community.**

About our books, visit:
www.treborarthurpublishing.com

Everyday Practical Leadership

Paper Version - ISBN: 978-0-9884957-4-6

To find more about Everyday Practical Leadership:

Google Search: **Everyday Practical Leadership**

Amazon: **Everyday Practical Leadership**

Web site: www.opportunitygrp.com

Everyday Practical Leadership

The leaders concrete guide to building winning teams delivering value-added results

Table of Contents

The pessimist complains about the wind. The optimist expects it to change.

The leader adjusts the sails.

John Maxwell

A LEADER TAKES PEOPLE WHERE THEY WANT TO GO. A GREAT LEADER TAKES PEOPLE WHERE THEY DON'T WANT TO GO BUT OUGHT TO BE.

ROSALYNN CARTER

Vulnerability is the birthplace of innovation, creativity and change. *Brene' Brown*

I sucked at leadership…

Notes:

It took me a long time to connect the dots as to why, and I will keep this short.

I loved and adored my 4th grade teacher, Mrs. 'R.' But in 10th grade I found out that Mrs. R had written in my file something along the lines of, *'Bob will never do well in life, he really isn't that smart.'*

So, the 9 year old boy who loved and adored her was crushed and the 15 year old sophomore who heard the news came out swinging to prove her wrong.

And for 30 years I proved her wrong in so many ways. I was a number one sales rep at multiple companies. I was a killer trainer. I was a hard core, win at all costs and drive my team to victory marketing manager.

And about 20 years ago a bell rang (ok, it was like a gong).

Because I was alone. I was 'right.' But I was alone. Sure, when a tough job arose, I got called. Because I came across as 'can-do, fearless, and full of fire'. And I would get the job done, on time and on budget.

But I was doing it alone.

In this book and on this page, I won't bore you with the details. And there are lots of them. Let's just say, that turning that corner 20 years ago helped me walk into a light that has fueled a passion in my heart that won't quit. A passion for helping people work for the right reasons, for reasons that bring fulfillment and peace to them and the people they care about.

So from the residue of a crushed heart, and from 30 years of fighting to prove I could succeed has emerged a recipe for winning that really works. As you read, you will see that this formula does not come from just me, it comes from a world of great thinkers, workers and leaders. To whom I am indebted.

Bit by bit the pieces have fallen into place to be 5 tenets that are easy to deploy.

My hope is that either here, or somewhere, you find ways to win and win with others in methods that make a positive difference for a world that needs good leaders.

May you find joy in your heart, fulfillment in your work and be an inspiration to all those around you!

Bob

In a Nutshell

The conscious leader's end game;
Attract, inspire and retain the right people.

You have more power at your fingertips than ever before, the question is:
'What are you going to do with it?' *Microsoft AI (message from Microsoft Artificial Intelligence)*

In a Nutshell

Notes:

Leadership? Let's just cut to the chase. It's all about winning.

Everyday Practical Leadership is about winning in a way you have never experienced before. Winning the way the best, brightest and richest in business win. Winning that enables short and long term success. Winning for your heart, and your mind, it will make your life easier, more fulfilling and reduce stress.

Winning at a level that once you start, you will never want to stop.

This book is not about management (although it will help you manage projects more effectively); it's about authentic leadership with impact. Leadership in a frenetically paced, globally connected, schizophrenic 'it's all about me' world. Clear, dynamic sharable leadership strategies and tactics you use every day.

First, let's be clear about the dichotomy between leadership and management. A Google® search delivers these two easy to understand definitions:

> Management is the administration of an organization[1.] or a process.

> Leadership is both a research area and a practical skill encompassing the ability of an individual or organization to "lead" or guide other individuals, teams, or entire organizations [2]. *Author note, the best 'guides' lead with a sense of curiosity.*

I don't know about you, but I have never met anyone who wanted to be 'managed.' We all prefer to be led. And we all want to win. Everyday Practical Leadership is about developing the practical skills of leadership and allowing you to grow (research and learning) as a person and leader on a constant basis (and your team also grows).

Understand, I am not bashing management. What I am saying is that you must be able to call up both your manager-self (administration) and your leadership-self (a curious guide) at will when required. We all need to manage things when the situation demands. And, to win, we have to practice leadership when the situation demands.

Meaning, you must be able to activate leadership at will. You must have at your mental disposal, embedded in your mind a leadership methodology and mind-set that works. But, as I write this, there are over 70,000 books on Amazon on leadership. You would think we have the conversation covered? So what is different here about Everyday Practical Leadership?

Management is doing things right; leadership is doing the right things. *Peter Drucker*

EPL is simple, actionable and sustainable. The power of EPL is it works at three levels. Let me explain. As I mentioned before, you want to win. Right? In business, love and war, we all want to win.

Go ahead, admit it. You want to win. And it's not just OK. It's expected. In fact, it's important to recognize, because winning enables these concepts around the higher level of leadership you will be exploring. And I don't ever want to work with a leader again who did not want to win (did it once, it was cumbersome).

Right now in the spheres of leadership development, the industry has created a divide in thinking, reducing our ability to win. Look at the landscape of theory, training and chatter there is emphasis around inclusion and collaboration and conflict avoidance. Yet, the bottom line for any of us leading a team is – we all have to win on multiple fronts. You have to deliver on your metrics or you are the first big loser (politically in your organization and maybe with losing your job).

Ok. So what do we do about it?

My team and I have been wrestling this core issue for some time. We facilitate a successful and popular transformational leadership experience in upstate NY. Through the prodding and help of some really great thinking, science and research, we spent time asking the question, 'What is the bigger question we need to be asking? What is the core question we are not considering in our approach to transformational leadership development?'

And the question began to take form from participants in the program, from executive sponsors and from ourselves, 'What makes me/us care about what you are doing?' It became obvious to us that the program we have is really good. And it's effective, from a transformational standpoint. But we had not been able to put our finger on the underlying aspect. Cognitively the program was on fire, yet something was missing from an emotional characteristic (and there is emotion in everything we do, although emotion is not the only thing).

Let me make it perfectly clear that our mission is to build leaders and enable them to find a high level of fulfillment successfully practicing outstanding leadership every day. We have graduated over 500 people (we call it, Developing Conscious Leadership), and there is a whole pile of success stories. But, there has been this nagging question about, 'What is the bigger real purpose of what we are doing?' Which meant, what is the core underlying intent of our work?

And this gets to the 3 levels mentioned above.

Notes:

Its not the load that breaks you down. It's the way you carry it!   *Lou Holtz*

A core answer emerged from clients, the facilitation team and from the universe of thinkers. It was not like a blinding light one day, the breakthrough was from an observation from a kind man who asked a critical question. He asked, 'Are you really in touch with your core intent? You seem to be skirting the real message. I don't know what it is, but you are not clear about it, I see it in your eyes.'[3]

We were to a degree in touch with our core intent through our mission and at the same time not outrageously clear about it. Not clear to the point that it rolled off our tongue with passion and sat comfortably with us in conversation.

What came to us (after curious discussion) is that the core intent and power of what is here has been baked into Everyday Practical Leadership (EPL) for some time. But clarity around the underlying intent of what EPL gives us has not had the light of day focused on it in a way that exposed its real power.

And that power is what this section opened with, but through our curious exploration has emerged to a message about leadership that requires 3 levels. And we are excited about it! Here it is:

To be effective, attractive and meaningful, the bottom line of successful leadership is simply this; **It has to be all about winning.**

But. This idea of <u>winning</u> needs an update since reality is, times have changed. The needs of people have changed and our understanding of how interdependently we operate in organizations has changed (note: this thinking includes the broad spectrum of organizations, including for profit, NGOs and government).[4]

In this updated view of winning we have three players who need to feel like winners:

1. You, the leader
2. Your team
3. Your Stakeholder community

And as the leader, if you want to win for the long term, you must be focused on creating an environment that works for all the players. This means all the players have to feel like they are winning at a level that is fair. We call it WIN3.

And with WIN3, you will attract, inspire and retain the best people to drive value for your Stakeholder community.

Let's decode this a bit…

Notes:

Life has meaning only in the struggle. *Stevie Wonder*

In summary, **WIN3** is:

1. **Win for me.**
   As the leader, I have to cognitively (logically and rationally) as well as emotionally understand that I am winning, or I just go to work, give all of myself and get burned out.

2. **Win for team.**
   As the leader, I have to inspire and enable a winning team, or the good people leave, the bad ones stay, we never taste victory, and it becomes a race to the bottom for talent and results. Winning teams are learning teams. They are creative and flexible. They can do anything!

3. **Win for Stakeholders.**
   As the leader, I have to create an environment of win/win/win with my Stakeholder community where all our respective critical needs are met and we all work together to serve each other to achieve a larger common good. This creates a sustainable long term business and organization.

We will get to details about enable WIN3. But right now, let's try an experiment. Invest 5 minutes and write down authentic answers to the following questions:

1. For **me** to feel like a long term winner, I need?

2. For **my team** to feel like they are winning on a regular basis they need?

3. For **my Stakeholder community** to be served well and their needs met, they need?

_____

_____

_____

_____

_____

_____

You can't connect the dots looking forward. You can only connect them looking backwards. Steve Jobs

Some people in the previous exercise answer none of these questions well. Some answer one or two. But, the answers are generally not deep, meaningful and most importantly, authentically inspirational.

The Everyday Practical Leadership process will help you to uncover your needs, as well as the needs of your team and Stakeholders. Once you understand these needs, you and your team can decide if you want to try and fill them.

Fulfilling a need for someone offers value. Fulfilling a need provides a benefit. And, if you are going to fulfill a need, in order to really provide value you must understand the need from the perspectives of both the giving and receiving parties (that creates win/win).

The Everyday Practical Leadership process takes all of that into account.

Bottom line is simply this - when my needs are met, I am happier, healthier and more engaged. I am in a position to be inspired. When I am part of an inspired team, I am for the long term energized, enthused and constantly learning. When I am inspired, I stay. When I am on a winning team, other winners are attracted to the team.

Enjoy the journey of this book and the Everyday Practical Leadership process. And, you may take solace in the fact that hundreds of people have come before, testing, refining and adding perspective to the process.

Now it's yours, own your leadership journey!

Notes:

Citations:

[1] https://en.wikipedia.org/wiki/Management

[2] https://en.wikipedia.org/wiki/Leadership

[3] This gentleman is Will Wise of 'From Me to We.' His book is: Ask Powerful Questions: Create Conversations That Matter, ISBN-13: 978-1545322994

[4] Firms of Endearment: How World-Class Companies Profit from Passion and Purpose (2nd Edition), by Raj Sisodia, Pearson FT Press; 2 edition (February 19, 2014), ISBN-13: 978-0133382594

[5] The surprising ingredient that makes businesses work better | Marco Alverà, TEDx, https://youtu.be/mgcjr1yz7ow

Executive Summary

Leadership: Attract, inspire and retain the right people to build win/win/win for your Stakeholder community.

Don't address their brains. Address their hearts. *Nelson Mandela*

A common view of business is it's a mix of people, process and technology. Technology is no longer the hurdle of days past. Good process is not a major obstacle - we have processes for everything. So why are we forced to push so hard and so often to achieve our desired outcomes?

We have not figured out the people part. And, the simple truth is, the people part is the hardest. Fraught with a myriad of difficult and frustrating variables.

Everyday Practical Leadership (EPL) gives you a roadmap for attracting, inspiring and retaining the best people. Not managing them, really leading them. And there is a bit of magic in EPL, the people who want to work, learn and win together (A-Team folks) will be attracted to your team. The C-Team folks will go away.

Let's begin by unraveling 'manage vs. lead'. We manage to a task or process. Leading might be described as - *Creating inspired cooperation and collaboration within my Stakeholder community generating high-value outcomes.* This fosters attracting, inspiring and retaining the right people. Let's decode your role in the long version, its powerful:

- **Create** – You don't do the work, you create the environment for success for the team to do the work. You have to create and build the desire for people to want to be interested to invest time and energy in the work.

- **Inspired** – You must have inspired teams of people tackling the complex issues facing your organization. People who are inspired can do anything (yes, anything). Inspired people will learn, experiment and push until they are successful. You must create inspired teams. Inspired teams are hard to manage, because they are on fire, for the right reasons. Inspired teams are inspired because they fulfill their YES!

- **Cooperation and collaboration** – This is critical, its how different views, skills and ideas become adopted for problem solving of complex situations. No one person has the answers. Its takes a team! This requires a dynamic team.

- **Stakeholder community** – Its no longer all about the employee or the customer, its about building balanced win/win/win within your wider Stakeholder community (Stakeholders include customers, vendors, partners, employees, investors and so forth, everyone you touch). In a balanced win environment, everyone gets what they need (not what they want).

- **Generating high-value outcomes** – Delivering real value to your Stakeholder community is what keeps people coming back. Your Stakeholders must see benefit in working with you over other available options.

  And what is a benefit? A benefit is something that solves a problem or satisfies a need for less cost (time, inconvenience, money) than if I did it myself (its why we buy food at a grocery store instead of raising it ourselves).

Leaders mindfully (on purpose and objectively) pay attention to the right things that matter to their team so the team is inspired. The next page explains the leadership strategy of the model, and its all about you for now.

Later we attend to the team.

'The soft stuff, is the hard stuff, that makes a difference.'   *Lee Cockrell, retired, GM Walt Disney World*

Over the years, clients have helped to refine the following leadership strategy. It's a simple model I call the **Conscious Leader** model. It is intended to help you determine what's important and what to pay attention to everyday in order to be an effective leader. Keep all three parts in mind constantly (think of a three legged stool, take off one leg and it just does not work, you fall down).

The philosophy is - this is simple. The strategy is - execute all three points consistently and reflect/learn as you progress (represented by   ).

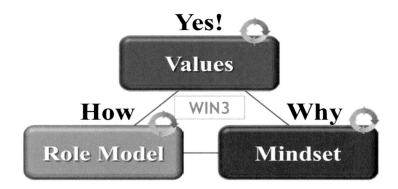

This is a brief explanation for each of the three Conscious Leader points (key points on the next page):

1. **Our YES!, what we are excited about *(Values):*** First of all, its 'we'. An inspired team shares the same goals. Not my goals or your goals, or the corporate goals. The team's goals. What we get excited about – Its about the value we bring to our Stakeholder community (the people we serve). We must understand who our Stakeholders are, what they need and share those stories – its our YES!

2. **How I show Up *(Role Model) impacts everyone:*** As a leader, to have an inspired team, I must pay attention to how I show up in every situation. Bottom line, if people fear me, they are in defense mode. I have to show up with trust and respect for everyone. I have to communicate well on a regular basis. When I run meetings and give presentations, people must leave inspired. No pass on these, ever.

3. **My Why *(Leadership Mindset) impacts my Yes and my How, I need to be in touch with it and bring it honor:*** This takes time and energy to develop. My core purpose, beliefs, values, motivations, fears (we all have them) and practice of Emotional Intelligence habits must be conscious and driving me to act as a leader in every situation. My 'Why' keeps me leading or derails me when stressed.

The philosophical aspect is WIN3. Leaders must feel like they are winning, set their teams up to feel like winners and enable their Stakeholders to feel like they are winning. Leaders enable people to generate a sense of dignity, embrace the pride of ownership and celebrate the joy of results. Winning has value, and keeps me coming back.

The next page explores specific nuances for each point of the triangle.

"Become the person who would attract the results you seek." *Jim Cathcart, author The Self-Motivation Handbook*

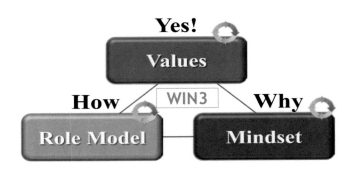

Find below more details about the Conscious Leadership model:

1. Our **YES!**, what <u>we</u> are excited about:
    *   **Stakeholder Needs** – High performing and inspired teams know who their core Stakeholders are and what they need. This leads to a sense of purpose.
    *   **Higher Purpose & Results** – The value we bring to our Stakeholders and winning business results.
    *   **Core Values, Shared Beliefs** – What we hold ourselves accountable to and the beliefs that we share.
    *   **Culture & Common Behaviors** – The type of culture we support and our common behaviors (such as expert or learning, asking questions…).

2. **How** I show Up *(Role Model)*
    *   **Trust & Respect** – Real leaders trust and respect all people.
    *   **Meetings & Presentations** – These represent us to each other and to the people who attend/watch them. All meetings and presentations have to generate enthusiasm, provide value and feed our Yes!
    *   **Goal Setting** – Everyone needs to know what is expected. Good goals give us a reason to show up well and help us know how to participate.
    *   **Communication & Interactions** – All leaders use every interaction as a means to inspire people, align them with purpose and remind them of their importance.

3. My **Why** *(Leadership Mindset)*
    *   **Beliefs & Values** – Supportive, positive & forward thinking.
    *   **Motivation(s)** – Focused on the potential and possibilities of all people.
    *   **Mindfulness** – Paying attention, on purpose, to what's really going on with a sense of curiosity (without judgement, until judgement is called for).
    *   **Emotional Intelligence** – Gaining and using information from emotions to always foster and develop better teams and relationships.

Everyday Practical Leadership enables Conscious Leadership to take action. For a step by step summary of the Everyday Practical Leadership model, find the page entitled **Winning Team – Playbook.**

Introduction
Welcome to Everyday Practical Leadership (EPL)

People will forget what you said, people will forget what you did, but people will never forget how you made them feel. *Maya Angelou*

Everyday Practical Leadership has its roots in the manufacturing and services sector. It grew up during the turbulent times of the 1990s when technology was expensive and difficult to use. The traditional role of the manager, organizational leader, and the conceptual framework and infrastructure of business came under pressure from multiple angles.

This unrelenting pressure comes from and continues to this day:

- Powerful international market movements (versus a local view)
- Rise of the power of the individual (social media, Google™)
- Ability for billions of people to participate in mass communication (Internet, Smart Phones, Artificial Reality, social media)
- Emerging consciousness that usurps old school business thinking (concepts such as the TEAL[1] paradigm)
- Constant, persistent and ever increasing integration of technology with real-time feedback into everything we do.

These forces and others are giving rise to a new type of business class and classlessness in a turbulent and fast moving world. Seems hopeless to some. But others see opportunity. The people who see opportunity are inspired!

Two sayings stick – the first <u>used</u> to be true; the other is the <u>cold</u> truth:

1. Henry Ford was supposedly known to say,

   'If I always do what I always did, I will always get what I always got.'

   That used to be true… But now, if I don't change, I lose. There is significant challenge in that old way of thinking, and if you think that way, you lose. The reality now: ***If I always do what I always did, the world will run right past me because things are changing so fast.***

2. The cold truth:

   The only means for success in an uncertain future is to **create my own future.** A future that has value to my YES, satisfies my WHY and allows me to show up in my authentic self (a leader's HOW).

   Everyday Practical Leadership enables you to create a successful future using the collective inspired power of your team and your Stakeholder community.

The inspired power of my team and Stakeholders!

Read on…

Notes:

'The thinking that created the situation we are in is not the thinking that will get us out of it.'
Albert Einstein

In history as we know it, the bosses and managers of an organization held the keys to knowledge, innovation and forward thinking. People worked hard for a paycheck. However technology, culture and the social norms of business have changed dramatically and every leader must grapple with the new truth of the team and the people who come into our employ, and it is;

All work is so complex anymore; only an inspired and engaged team can truly create effective and efficient solutions for conquering the problems that face them, or build opportunities where your Stakeholders find value.

It does not matter what business you are in, whether it is running a beauty salon or overseeing thousands of people in high tech manufacturing operations; **the only hope you have for long term success is in the inspiration and engagement of your team.** Examples of success surround us – Google, Uber/Lyft, AirBNB, Amazon, Tesla, Apple, and now coming back strong, Microsoft.

The task for inspiration falls on you, the leader. The team <u>wants</u> you to inspire them. They want you to set them on fire so they can do a great job and make a difference in the world in which they choose to participate. They will put their energy somewhere. It might as well be in building a successful future on <u>your</u> team.

The research is clear, people want autonomy, mastery and purpose.[2]

EPL is an interdependent leadership system that inspires by taking into account such vital elements as:
- People's desire to achieve, learn and grow
- An individual's desire for autonomy mastery and purpose
- Overcoming the fears that get in our way
- The incredible power of peer pressure
- And much more…

Everyday Practical Leadership gives you the formula for this success! I wrote this book and have believed in and refined this process for over 20 years for only one reason – to help people succeed. To help hardworking people find their YES and find true joy. We have a world that is amazing, but few people find real true joy – I hope you are one of us.

Bob Freese

[1] Reinventing Organizations by Frederic Laloux, ISBN-13: 978-2960133509
[2] Drive: The Surprising Truth About What Motivates Us, D. Pink, ISBN: 978-1594484803

Notes:

'There is something inside you that is greater than any obstacle'   *Christian Larson*

Notes:

In the very early 1990s I was the marketing director for an outsourcing organization. We were growing at a rate of about $30M per year and in some sectors, we were awesome. In others, well, we had our operational challenges.

One day, an operational expert came into our midst as a calm, humble gentleman. His name was Bill Gooding.

Bill would drop into any operational site where we were having problems and challenges (including employee retention, customer satisfaction, cost over-runs and meeting service level agreements).

He was able to cut the workforce and labor cost at least in half, change and update the technology and improve client relationships at a tremendous level. He also drove significant organizational and corporate results turning that site into profitable operations (in fact very very profitable), he achieved incredible results.

This was the kicker though, after Bill had been at a site for a few months and had made all these changes, the clients, the vendors, and the employees loved him! Even after all of the changes he had brought about, those people were ready to walk through fire at any time to support Bill and their team.

I went to meet Bill. From a marketing standpoint, we had to find out what his secret was so we could duplicate it throughout the organization and make his operating philosophy part of our differentiating message. And in his humble way, when I asked him what his secret process was, he replied, "What process?"

Bill and I invested time talking about his beliefs, philosophies and views. Over time, the original Everyday Practical Leadership model emerged. Back then, we simply called it Practical Leadership. The addition of 'Everyday' is merely because in order to be successful with this system, you have to use it every-day.

That dear reader, is a critical aspect of the success formula here:
Use all five tenets every day.

No more, no less, just follow the recipe as it is laid out.

When you follow Everyday Practical Leadership, you will create engagement and more importantly inspiration. We look at inspiration as a higher form of engagement.

Think of it, when you are inspired, you are willing to take risks. You see opportunity when others see issues. When you are inspired, you are excited, pumped up, creative and full of ideas to solve problems, create opportunities. Think of the power of having your team inspired everyday! Authentic leaders have a core belief:

Inspiration creates value!

Players win Games. Teams win Championships.
Successful coaches know they are coaching with every word and gesture they use. All the time!

Notes:

But – wait! I don't want to be tied to a strict process!

Don't worry, you aren't tied to a strict process, you are engaged in an interdependent system to inspire your team.

Look at it this way, imagine you are a chef. A chef has a recipe. But great chefs always improvise a little. A pinch here, a pinch there. When a recipe is new, they follow it to the letter. Once they are comfortable, they get creative. You can do the same here. Follow the process, learn from it, then get creative and start serving up highly valuable outcomes to your Stakeholder community that make a difference. That difference will come in many forms:

- Reduced costs
- Faster achievement of short and long term goals
- Creating thinking on the part of your team

And, like anyone, you have to have a goal. The goal Bill Gooding had was clear and easy to understand, and in this complex world, it really becomes the goal of successful leadership. As the leader, its not your job to do the work, it is your job to remove obstacles and barriers to success. Your goal is to:

**Attract, inspire and retain the right people on your team generating
high-value outcomes for my Stakeholders!**

Ponder the above statement for a moment. The word 'attract' means people come along of their own fruition. 'Inspired' generates creativity and energy and a Can Do attitude. 'Retain' creates value from the whole is greater than the sum of the parts. 'Stakeholder' is the broad expanse of the places where you make a difference and 'high-value' is what makes a difference for people because with our Stakeholders, we must provide more than a transaction of we are to be successful for the long term.

You will have many options to choose from as you embark on the Everyday Practical Leadership journey. The only option you cannot take is to skip a tenet. By skipping a tenet you will create your own living hell. I have had many clients fall in love with one of the powerful concepts contained in EPL, and their team soon turns sour on them. Maybe you are living that now (like trying to rake water uphill alone – it just does not work, and you can't be successful for the long term).

Because like cooking, you have to have all the basic ingredients in the mix, or it tastes like cheap dog food.

Lets get started! See if Everyday Practical Leadership is for you, answer the diagnostic.

Oh – the questions might need some deep thinking, be brutally honest with your answers and give yourself some time to think about your answers.

The secret of getting ahead is getting started. *Mark Twain*

Origins of the EPL diagnostic: I sat attentively in Paul's office listening while he lamented issues facing his operation with 500+ people. Cost overruns, equipment malfunctions, overtime out of control and union labor disputes topped the list. It was not a pretty picture. Paul was prepared to fire, relocate and downgrade people. He was fired up mad and ready to 'pull the trigger' to send a heavy message that he was not going to tolerate this shoddy level of operation any longer.

It was uncomfortable in that room. Uncomfortable for me, my partner and Paul's executive team who felt their necks on the chopping block. This list of challenges had been brewing for a long time, not uncommon.

Paul handed us a gift that day. What Paul craved was a clear and concise understanding on 'how he was going to win.' I did not have it for him and it became evident I had a gap in the process. Eventually, over the course of a couple of years, the gift of that need emerged for all of us to use, and is on the next page, the EPL Diagnostic.

As we positioned the EPL process for Paul that warm afternoon, he only saw three things:
1. Losing control to his team – he really liked control, he liked being 'right'
2. Tenet # 3 - Achieving Results – he loved keeping score so he could prove to people he was right
3. A lack of bottom line – he did not see the big picture in a way that made sense. He could not get his head around getting started. He told me, 'this is not intuitive'. He wanted more hard and fast rules (to enforce).

However, through his frustration and angst, something clicked and finally, with a sense of resignation he said; 'this is bigger than me and us in this room.' We all talked for a long time about theory and goals and ideas.

Eventually, and to his credit, Paul handed responsibility to one of his chiefs and let her run with the program. Paul made a good choice, because Cheryl was not only smart, she was strategic, loved to win and wanted one thing more than anything. Cheryl wanted to leave a legacy. Unbeknown to anyone in the room, in five years, Cheryl would own a small fishing boat off the New England coast and retire in a comfortable bungalow.

How does it end? Within a year, a highly technical team, running interdependent complex 24/7 mission critical operations that included multiple union, partner and multifaceted Stakeholder relationships achieved:
1. Avoidance of a $1M mechanical overhaul because a maintenance team took on a major challenge and proved the experts wrong
2. Reduction of supply costs below industry average (they now rate in the top 10% of their industry)
3. Improvement of Stakeholder relationships on many fronts, including no labor relation issues for over 3 years (since we last checked in).

The diagnostic on the next page focuses on your team and how your team works. EPL engagement includes Stakeholders, however this diagnostic is more focused on team engagement, operations, dynamics and inspiration.

Our goal from your diagnostic's results is you have a clearer understanding of what you will achieve when engaging the 5 tenets of EPL with your team(s). If you have multiple teams, make copies and diagnose each one.

One client suggested we create a Team Diagnostic so the leader can gain feedback from the team. We might do that over time. However, if you are not sure of an answer to any of the topics, then your team is not sure either. And that, for you, is a sure sign that changes need to get underway.

Go ahead, take a few minutes to complete the diagnostic. Be honest, be truthful and we hope you find value in getting started.

The Everyday Practical Leadership Diagnostic

EPL isn't for everyone. Your answers to this diagnostic, and score you generate helps you determine the value of the system for you and your team (if you have a larger organization with many teams reporting up to you, replace the words 'My team' with 'All my teams', or complete multiple copies).

"Prescription without diagnosis is malpractice."
Dr. Will Sparks, Dennis Thompson Chair, Leadership, McColl School of Business at Queens University of Charlotte

This diagnostic focuses on your team and how your team works. Even though EPL engagement includes Stakeholders, this diagnostic is more focused on your team's engagement, operations, dynamics and inspiration.

	Question	Strongly Agree		Ambivalent *or* Not Sure		Strongly Disagree
1	Our team's results exceed expectations on a regular basis. In our space, we could be 'the benchmark'	5	4	3	2	1
2	My team brings me prioritized, high value opportunities and goals on a consistent basis (vs. I tend to see & bring opportunities)	5	4	3	2	1
3	My team clearly understands who comprises our internal and external core stakeholder community (ies)	5	4	3	2	1
4	My team appreciates and often articulates the needs of our core stakeholders (not from the team's perspective, but from the direct perspective of the stakeholders)	5	4	3	2	1
5	At the end of every day or shift, my team is clearly proud of the work they have accomplished & the value created	5	4	3	2	1
6	My team engages in various forms of continuous learning on a regular basis, driving greater wisdom in all operations	5	4	3	2	1
7	My team attracts and keeps A-players	5	4	3	2	1
8	At all levels, my team engages in positive peer pressure and support, focusing on the team win (vs. individual stars)	5	4	3	2	1
9	My team holds themselves accountable, on purpose, for the right priorities on an ongoing basis and we deliver on-time	5	4	3	2	1
10	We have fun at work and feel like we are winners	5	4	3	2	1
11	We know, articulate and live by a clear set of team developed Core Values, shared beliefs and common behaviors	5	4	3	2	1
12	I have a personal relationship with all my team members, to the level of knowing and understanding them as a person	5	4	3	2	1
13	Everyone on my team values each other's strengths; actively supports each other to meet core stakeholder needs	5	4	3	2	1
14	My team is a 'safe place' where not knowing all the answers is ok, because the team is there to develop and build the answers	5	4	3	2	1
15	I actively pay attention to opportunities for team training, tools and support and am clear on what they need to keep winning	5	4	3	2	1

My Score _____

Diagnostic - Impact

Through experience and working with 100's of people, the indicators below may seem on target or not. Think about what is going on and not going on in your organization. You will probably, upon reflection agree with the findings.

Vulnerability is the birthplace of innovation, creativity and change.
Dr. Brene' Brown, TED, Listening to Shame

Diagnostic Summary: Any score below 80% indicates you are probably frustrated and looking for answers. The Everyday Practical Leadership model will help you align your energy with superior results in all aspects of a high performing team. Send a note to: bobfreese@gmail.com or call 585-671-4400 to get started.

Score	Remarks
75 – 60 80% or higher (all your answers in the 4 or 5 range)	Most likely practicing good leadership. Indicates you most probably lead (vs. manage) your team and long term success is attainable. You are meeting the needs of your team, supporting them well and they are focused on the right priorities. Everyday Practical Leadership can help you put into place a more formal process for gaining improved results, inspired team members and developing increased levels of team wisdom. Scoring rationale: Leadership is not a guessing game. Successful leaders base resources, time and energy on enabling success and know where to focus. Any answer on the diagnostic below a 4 indicates you are 'not sure' and 'not sure' is not effective or acceptable for leadership.
59 – 50 79 – 66% (some answers in the 4 or 5 range, some in 3 or less)	You are practicing some leadership, however often feel frustrated. You as a leader mostly 'get it' but are unfulfilled and most likely tired of 'raking water uphill alone.' This score indicates areas of importance to team members where their needs are not satisfied (and these may be unconscious or hard to articulate to you or by you). You may not be aware of the elements you are missing. We have found that leaders in this score range are most likely frustrated from: • Results that meet expectations most of the time, but it's a regular and constant struggle • Inability to attract and keep the A players you need to truly be successful • You get the work done, but the level of inspirational creativity on the team to fix short term issues and long term vision is lacking and requires a lot of push/energy • Probably more issues and challenges not listed above… Everyday Practical Leadership can become your guidebook, enabling your team's success in the above points and more. EPL will get your team fired up without you to giving 127% all the time. Scoring rationale: Leadership is not a guessing game. Successful leaders base resources, time and energy on enabling success and know where to focus. Any answer on the diagnostic below a 4 indicates you are 'not sure' and 'not sure' is not effective or acceptable for leadership.
49-15 65% or below (most answers in the 3 or below range)	You are practicing some leadership, however you are often frustrated or not sure what to do. There are areas of importance to team members where their needs are not satisfied. You are not paying attention to what we know matters to the long term success of high performing teams. This score indicates you have work to do in building an environment of engagement, inspiration and *esprit-de-corps* where people create long term value-added success. You most likely suffer from: • Results that are not up to expectations on a regular basis, no matter how hard you try • Lack of inspiration and team growth through learning – you repeat issues over and over • Not able to attract and keep the level of talent needed to stay competitive or ahead. • More issues and challenges… Everyday Practical Leadership can become your guidebook enabling your team's success in the above points and more. You need to pay attention to all five tenets, patiently roll out the program. Scoring rationale: Leadership is not a guessing game. Successful leaders base resources, time and energy on enabling success and know where to focus. Any answer on the diagnostic below a 4 indicates you are 'not sure' and 'not sure' is not effective or acceptable for leadership.

FAQs

Think Different!
Apple's slogan in 1997, 10 years before they launch the first iPhone - good things take some time...

1. **What is Everyday Practical Leadership (EPL)?**

   This is an easy to implement, team based system that builds winning teams (not in sports, but in business). This system drives inspiration, learning, accountability, planning, goals, and collaboration within your team and Stakeholder community. The end result is an inspired team that requires less direct intervention on your part for driving high-value outcomes within your Stakeholder community (in fact, you will intervene much less).

2. **What is my Stakeholder Community?**

   Simply this; businesses operate as interdependent entities. We have employees, customers, partners, shareholders, investors and more. In building a Stakeholder community, we must learn to work within the interdependent nature of all of the people and organizations we touch. The basic rule is; no decision is made for the benefit of one Stakeholder to the detriment of another, thereby creating virtuous cycles of win-win and long term success.

3. **How do I execute Everyday Practical Leadership?**

   For your team, the **Winning Team – Playbook** is a handout for you to use with your team. Use it verbatim. However, if you need to change it, go ahead. One aspect of EPL is that it is totally transparent. You can share all the materials and instructions with anyone on your team. Remember, transparency creates trust. For you, the leader, the **Winning Team - Playbook** is your step-by-step guide to implementation. Follow all the tenets, in order and do not skip any. You keep repeating tenets 1-5, over and over (often in parallel).

4. **What are the benefits of using Everyday Practical Leadership?**
   You will build winning teams that…

   A. **Create real Stakeholder value & results -** In just a few weeks, your team will be achieving new goals maybe never before been considered, and these goals are based on driving Stakeholder value.

   B. **Are proud of their work -** Your teams will be proud of the work they accomplish, they will know the difference they make in the world and how they add value.

   C. **Engage in continuous learning -** The tenets are designed to drive learning within the team. This helps people grow, which is paramount to attracting, inspiring and retaining the right people in today's society.

   D. **Employ creative collaboration -** Since the only way to win is for the team to win, there is an esprit-de-corps (*a feeling of pride, fellowship, and common loyalty*) that emerges as the program rolls forward.

   E. **Provides positive peer pressure and support -** Instead of high flyers winning all the time and receiving all the accolades, everyone pulls their weight and helps each other succeed. The team wins. No individual wins.

   F. **Drives accountability across the entire team -** The team keeps score of their performance, results are obvious and clear. No one can hide any longer, and no one needs to hide. You are team building.

   G. **Enjoy a feeling of accomplishment and have fun -** Everyone wants to win and feel successful. EPL helps people feel like winners and they will know what and how they are winning.

   H. **Retain the best players and grow learners -** EPL automatically attracts winners and workers. The people who do not want to be accountable, will exit.

   I. **Attract 'A-Team' players -** The truth is, A players want to work with A players. They are willing to

'Its hard to beat someone who never gives up.' Babe Ruth

work with B players who want to learn. However A players will not tolerate C players very long.

The unfortunate reality is, traditional management functions and techniques tend to discriminate against A players and a team ends up with a group of C players wondering what's going on and with frustrated

leadership that can't seem to get enough done. Winning teams attract A players. You have no control over that, it's just reality. What you have control over is creating a winning team of inspired people.

Unless you are engaging at the A player level, you are attracting C players, frustrating and losing A & B players and you are participating in a 'race to the bottom' for talent.

5.   What are the pitfalls of Everyday Practical Leadership (EPL)?

The hardest thing for most managers is to 'let go' and 'let them.' EPL is a leadership system that demands the team takes over and works together. If you are the kind of manager who is directive, a micromanager or perfectionist, you may find this system uncomfortable. Learning takes time and people need to make mistakes to learn. People need to be in learning mode in order to be engaged and inspired. Leaders know that, many managers don't. We will explore this in detail later.

Remember, your job as a leader is to create an inspirational environment where learning, collaboration and results dominate. You are in charge of and accountable to creating the inspiration for the people who produce results. **Your job is not to do the work.** Your job is to help the people who do the work be successful.

Look at it this way – try EPL as an experiment and see how it goes. You can always go back to the old way if necessary. *Give it a month, then decide.* But give it a real month.

6.   How do I get started?

Follow the **Winning Team - Playbook.** Plan each tenet, let the system roll out at a pace the team can assimilate. Be mindfully conscious of everything you do (means: objectively pay attention, on purpose to what is going on). Give the Team a copy of the 'Winning Team – Playbook' or create your own.

CAUTION: Feel free to customize Everyday Practical Leadership. However, do <u>not </u>leave out any of the five tenets or you will **fail**.

7.   Why is the Playbook called 'Winning Team'?

Feedback. Everybody wants to win. The playbook needs to be for the team, not just the leader. This entire book is your playbook. The Winning Team Playbook is a page you might copy and share with your team.

8.   What is the significance of the star symbol?

A star has five points. Take a point away, and you have a blob. Same with Everyday Practical Leadership. For EPL, follow all five tenets or it does not work. If you want to win, follow the basic rules and you will win big. Cut corners, you lose. We have learned this in implementing EPL over and over and over.

9.   Why does Everyday Practical Leadership work?

EPL engages people at a visceral, rational and emotional level. This is not top down directive management, purely cognitive management or inside out thinking. This is how to implement the give and take of what fires people up and inspires them to be great. EPL aligns with research, psychology and motivational thinking.

Winning Playbooks - Introduction
A summary for the Everyday Practical Leadership model

If you don't think you're a winner, you don't belong here. Vince Lombardi

This page summarizes the tenets and steps of EPL for you. What follows are two summaries, one for you, the leader and one for the team. The more detailed page (next page - The Winning Leader Playbook) lists steps for you to follow. The Winning Team playbook is for the whole team. The rest of this book is built to help you execute each of the tenets and deal with the nuances of the system.

Remember, your end game is:
**Attract, inspire and retain the right people to build
win/win/win for your Stakeholder community (build value).**

Use the Winning Team - Playbook as a guide for team members (copy it, print it, share it). Solicit feedback, be flexible and honor the change cycle[1]. Implementing EPL can take some time, so be planful and patient.

Use this process every day to create ongoing forward progress. Have fun, support each other and learn.

Tenets	Summary of each Tenet
1. Building Enthusiasm	To be inspired or engaged in my work, I have to care about it. This tenet takes you and your team through a safe and motivating process of figuring out your YES; why you care about each other and what you do. Skip this tenet and what your organization does (your YES), for 67% [2] of your employees is just work.
2. Conditions for Victory (CFV)	Everyone must know, empirically what it means to win, or they really don't know how to fully participate or if what they do matters. This tenet gives the power of winning at elements that serve your YES, discovered above, over to your team. Skip this tenet and you will forever be the one coming up with answers (vs. your team inspired to create a better future).
3. Achieving Results	All teams want to know the score. This tenet puts scoring in the hands of the team and helps them to know they are winning. Skip this tenet and you lose A players that want to win, B players that want to learn and you keep C players that you don't want (it becomes a race to the bottom for talent).
4. Enabling Success	The tools and training to do the job are required to win. This tenet takes a unique look at this often 'assumed' process. Skip this tenet and your team is powerless to deliver results.
5. Developing Wisdom	Sharing our learning as a team helps us grow. This tenet supports team growth and learning by use of a safe 'Continuous Improvement' process. Skip this tenet and you will repeat mistakes, never build (or rebuild) a sense of 'team' and be caught in a cycle of slow regression to failure.

[1] The best and clearest 'change cycle' we have found is well covered in the book, **Transitions: Making Sense of Life's Changes**, published by Da Capo Lifelong Books, written by Dr. William Bridges, ISBN-13: 978-0738209043. We have been delivering 'Change Management' workshops for 20 years using Bridges model, and it works. One key point to remember is that all change equals some sort of loss (just accept that) and when you bring change, some people may push back. EPL minimizes the pushback through feedback loops that engage the team – but you will still get some pushback. Think of the pushback as 'feedback' and be open to it, because when people are pushing back, they are engaged.

[2] Reference - Gallup State of the American Workplace study, 2017

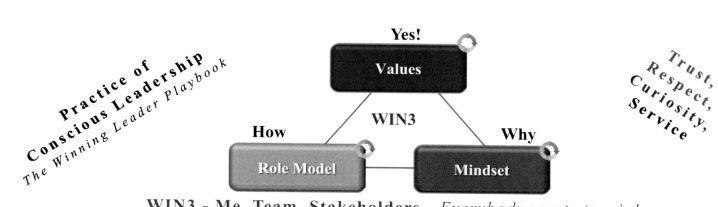

WIN3 - Me, Team, Stakeholders - *Everybody wants to win!*

Trust, Respect, Curiosity, Service

Meet people where they are and treat them the way they need to be treated.

There is no comfort in the growth zone and there is no growth in the comfort zone.

Tenets of Everyday Practical Leadership (EPL)	Tools & Actions
Planning & preparation ❖ **I am always a Role Model and leading**	1. Finish EPL Diagnostic & Strategic Plan 2. Engage right people in a Change Plan
1. Building Enthusiasm ❖ **We are all Role Models** –every interaction ❖ **Know Core Stakeholders** ❖ **Know and share Stakeholder Needs** ❖ **Play to our Higher Purpose, Shared Core Values, Beliefs & Behaviors**	1. Team held and shared Stakeholder (SH) conversations & stories (appx 2) 2. Use core values, beliefs, behaviors priority sheets (appx 4) 3. Develop team's Higher Purpose (appx 2) 4. Vision boards (team and individual)
2. Conditions for Victory (CFV) ❖ **Team built S.M.A.R.T. goals** (step goals are OK) ❖ **Stakeholder & higher purpose focused**	1. Build <u>team</u> goals based on SH needs, use S.M.A.R.T. goals (appx 5) 2. Team goal is 'research,' indicates perspective of the team 3. Choose a date for Tenet #5
3. Achieving Results ❖ **Team developed scoring & updating** ❖ **Visual and public scoreboard** ❖ **Only team can win** (not individuals)	1. Team decides how to keep score and team performs the scorekeeping (gamify) 2. The scoreboard is public, update daily 3. Everyone must achieve results or the team has no celebration in #5
4. Enabling Success ❖ **Supportive practices & policies** ❖ **Deliver actionable tools & learning** ❖ **Tap internal stars where possible**	1. Change any policy that deters success 2. Look intently for tools and training needed by team for a win (coach) 3. Delegate training to internal stars where possible (and set them up for success)
5. Developing Wisdom ❖ **Review-Right / Wrong / Different / How** ❖ **Celebrate TEAM wins** (not individuals) ❖ **Learning & growth is what we all want**	1. Remind team of session @ least 24 hours in advance in writing (for preparation) 2. Celebrate only if score is achieved 3. Facilitate the wisdom session no matter what happens – drive learning & growth

Ensure Everyone Feels Valued

Build Trusted Relationships

Practice Psychological Safety

Tenets & Guiding Principles	Activities to support the Tenets and Guiding Principles
1. Building Enthusiasm ❖ Role Models ❖ Core Stakeholders ❖ Stakeholder Needs ❖ Higher Purpose ❖ Shared Core Values, Beliefs & Behaviors	1. Agree we are a team and we represent ourselves and each other all the time 2. Map Core Stakeholders as a team (the ones we focus on) 3. Team members meet with Stakeholders and report on Stakeholder Needs[1] 4. Produce a set of Team Core Values[2] – what we commit to, what we stand for 5. Generate a team set of 'Beliefs & Behaviors' to support Core Values 6. Create Team Vision Board – where we are going, values, beliefs, behaviors 7. Develop Team Higher Purpose based on Stakeholder Needs and Core Values
2. Conditions for Victory (CFV) ❖ Team Built Goals ❖ Stakeholder & Higher Purpose Focused ❖ S.M.A.R.T. Goals	1. Team creates a S.M.A.R.T. Goal based on Stakeholder Needs honoring Higher Purpose, Core Values and Beliefs 2. Goal time should be 2 – 4 weeks out, no longer 3. Set the date for #5 – Developing Wisdom (and how you will celebrate) 4. Goal must have everyone involved – no one person/few can carry the team • S.M.A.R.T. - *Simple	Measurable	Attainable	Realistic	Time-Bound* (see Appendix 5 for more details)
3. Achieving Results ❖ **Team Developed Scoring & Updating** ❖ **Visual and Public** ❖ **Only Team Can Win**	1. Team determines how to score the Conditions for Victory and team members do the scorekeeping (not the leader) 2. Tracking must be visual and public on how each team member and the team are tracking toward CFV 3. Only the team wins, no person or group carries the team
4. Enabling Success ❖ Supportive Practices & Policies ❖ Actionable Tools ❖ Education	1. Leader must ensure that organizational practices, policy, and procedures are supportive of the Conditions for Victory 2. The Team requests tools and education necessary to meet the CFV 3. Leader searches for tools and education to enable victory – ask the questions, 'What do we need for victory? What is in our way?' 4. Training comes from inside expertise as often as possible 5. Remind team of the date for #5 – Developing Wisdom
5. Developing Wisdom ❖ **Review** ❖ **Celebration** ❖ **Learning**	1. Before the session, remind team members to bring thoughts around R/W/D/H or C/S/S/H to the session in writing. 2. Invite Stakeholders to be involved in these sessions whenever possible 3. Use the Parking Lot with Post-Its during the session (stay on target) 4. Run the review session using R/W/D/H (Right/Wrong/Different/How) or C/S/S/H (Continue/Stop/Start/How[3]) 5. Celebration only occurs when the team goal(s) is achieved – we honor effort and celebrate success

[1] Use a free Survey Monkey account to gather data, www.SurveyMonkey.com, see Appendix 3 for details
[2] Create a Wordle at: http://www.wordle.net/create Requires JAVA supported browser (Not Chrome)
[3] Scaling Up: How a Few Companies Make It... (Rockefeller Habits 2.0), Vern Harnish, ISBN: 978-0986019524

Being busy does not always mean real work. The object of work is production or accomplishment; to either of these ends there must be system, planning, intelligence, and honest purpose, as well as perspiration. Thomas Edison

Use these planning pages to get started. This first section is the bigger picture, the next section is more detailed for implementing change. Completing this planning may take some time and require feedback from Stakeholders (including your boss) and your team. This planning is meant to help you clarify for the nearer future where you will focus your efforts. Writing this down will enable you to clearly focus your team and Stakeholder on goals. Don't end up being too specific, that is for your team(s) to accomplish. You are setting direction.

Note: this planning will require more room to write than is provided on these two pages

1. In big picture terms, what I (the leader) want to accomplish over the next 12 months. This is your Yes! This is what is driving you now. It could be efficiency, learning, a new launch… *Getting in touch with your Yes! in public will help illuminate for you your 'Why.' Your Why is very important, because people will get a sense for your Why and will either be inspired by it or discouraged.*

_____

2. How the above aligns to my team's (or organization's) higher purpose, core values, beliefs. *Remember – alignment of principles is required for inspiration on your team.* How does what you want to accomplish align with your organization's strategy (this is important if you want support from the organization or you might be branded as a rebel)? You must be able to clearly articulate this alignment for people to want to get on board[1].

_____

3. Strategically, (using metrics as well as concepts [concepts are interesting, metrics are understandable]), accomplishing this goal means to me, my team and our Stakeholders. *Remember, people want to win, during change, there are many possible losses that could be present in the minds of your team(s). Laying out wining thinking gives people a reason to promote new ideas vs. adopt thinking that protects the old way.*

_____

4. Stakeholders who are impacted? *This can indicate to you the size and scope of your desires. Often, the answer to this question will bring in other parties who need to be there at the beginning. Getting people in on the ground floor is much easier and more effective thank having them catch up later.*

_____

5. Stakeholder needs and expectations? *This is the telling question. You may have a great idea, and without driving value for your Stakeholder community, you will be raking water uphill alone. The most successful leaders are the ones who listen to Stakeholders and 'hear' what they need (reference Steve Jobs and the soft screen on the iPhone).*

_____

6. What is causing this challenge, what is in the way? *Why do you need to do something different? Every problem is an opportunity, however, most people does not see opportunity, they only see problems. Carefully explaining why this change is necessary will help people get on board.*

_____

continued on the next page…

7. My real motivations for this project are…? *Be really honest with yourself here, because you have to carry your story with you. If you want something to succeed because you want to make a pile of money, so be it. However, people will sense this, the collective sees through a façade. Be honest here, maybe write a different story in the next item.*

_____

8. What would inspire people to adopt this and get behind it? *Projects and ideas driving real Stakeholder value have a much higher chance for adoption and support. Think of it this way, if you can guide a team to success, you just might accomplish what you wrote above. If you have to do it yourself, your odds of coming out big are minimal. Yes, its ok to want to own an island in the South Pacific. However, very few people get there alone. So go ahead, dig in, find inspiration for your team or organization and they when people are willing to walk through fire for you, you are on your way.*

_____

_____
_____
_____
_____
_____

[1] A note about strategic alignment with your company. If your plans are not clearly aligned with the organization's strategy, you are going to have a tough time finding energy for the long term to really accomplish the things you want to accomplish (satisfying your YES!). This is because deep down, your WHY will not be fulfilled and your work becomes just work. Or, if you need to change your organization, remember that is a really tough challenge, but often worth it. In the work we have done on culture change, it is most often a 3 – 5 year endeavor and requires a lot of planning, patience and energy. Everyday Practical Leadership works for a team or a whole company and remember, the company is made up of working teams and the tenets of EPL apply to each team. EPL is inclusive and participatory at the working team level.

> The most difficult thing is the decision to act, the rest is merely tenacity. The fears are paper tigers. You can do anything you decide to do. You can act to change and control your life; and the procedure, the process is its own reward.   *Amelia Earhart*

A goal is a dream with a deadline.   *Napoleon Hill*

The 'Change Planner' on the next two pages has morphed over the years from intense and sometimes very emotionally charged feedback by Stakeholders. And, you might have ideas on how to make it better. If you do, we want to hear from you.

There is huge value in paying attention to planning for success when it comes to change.   As mentioned earlier on the Summary page, the research and writings by Dr. William Bridges ring true for understanding change. And, there is a lot more good work available that encompasses how to bring about change.

Wait! I thought I was inspiring my team? Yes, and to do that, changes will have to come about. Some small, some big. To help you win at the task of making the changes you want to make, we have carefully crafted and molded the next page (and the guidance on the following page).

Here is the deal. When changing things for people, we are asking them to put aside what they know. And what they know is how to do their job and win. You want to improve that, and that means entering the great void of the unknown. For some its exciting. For some, its downright scary. Bottom line, all change is loss (#11 on the next page). Realizing that this is true helps you to understand people's reactions more clearly.

I have had folks get downright angry at the prospect of changing a process (such as 'What part of NO don't you understand?'). Developing the plan on the next page (including having people participate in plan development) has helped many times to pave the way for hugely successful projects.

One item to pay attention to is #18, Pilot or trial program, (get started, run an experiment). This is the brain child of Rich Sheridan of Menlo Innovations in Michigan (read his book, Joy, Inc., How To Build A Workplace People Love, ISBN: 978-1591847120). At dinner one night, Rich and I dove into change and how scary it is and he said, 'Running an experiment is safe. It allows for mistakes and learning and allows people to focus on the outcome vs. the loss.'

Rich runs an successful software company and takes his team and clients through some very extensive change often. We added his thought. And over time, what we have found is this: *Run experiments often. It keeps us open the feedback the learning and the possibilities of what is going on.*

Do yourself and everyone a favor. Plan for change. Involve others in the planning. Take some time to help yourself, you team and your Stakeholders win.

You will be happy you did it.

Notes:

Failing to plan is planning to fail. *Alan Lakein*

This is a planning tool for implementing change. Definitions and guidance for each line appear on the next page. This page encompass the realm of topics needed to be successful when implementing change. They are critical!

#	Topic	Notes, Dates, Action Items, Owners, Status…
1	Project Name:	
2	Start Date / End Date:	
3	Budget *($, time, ppl, tech., work that needs to stop, be outsourced or put on hold)*:	
4	Current State *(specific, measurable for clarity)*:	
5	Level of Change *(Incremental, Developmental, Transformational)*:	
6	Desired State *(Vision & S.M.A.R.T. Goals)*:	
7	Rationale for the Change *(why, hard / soft savings, alignment to YES!)*:	
8	Stakeholders Impacted:	
9	Stakeholder Needs *(now & after the change)*:	
10	Others Who May Need to Know & Why *(and when they should be told)*:	
11	Losses by those affected *(refer to DISC Styles, ALP Shadow Fears)*:	
12	Change Leadership/Executive Team:	
13	Executive & Investment Support Needed *(Time/Money/ Politics)*:	
14	Communication Vehicles & Tactics *(make messaging repeatable)*:	
15	Role Modeling - To Do's for leaders	
16	Guiding Team / Thought Leaders - *Actors (Early Adopters, Change Leaders)*:	
17	Change Implementation Team – *Detailers (Details, Project Mgmt.)*:	
18	Pilot or trial program *(get started, run an experiment)*:	
19	Anticipated Obstacles & Restraining Forces *(create a list from Stakeholder discussions)*:	
20	Success / Adoption Checkpoints & Metrics:	
21	Team & Individual Goals, Scoring Strategies:	
22	Tools, Training & Education Required *(account for super-users to luddites)*	
23	Review and Recognition (celebration) Process, Dates *(90 day max)*:	

Definitions and guidance for the topics of the Change Plan on the previous page.

#	Topic	Notes, Dates, Action Items, Owners, Status…
1	Project Name:	Common words Stakeholders understand. Avoid TLAs (three letter acronyms).
2	Start Date / End Date:	Most planning should not exceed 90 days
3	Budget *($, time, ppl, tech., work that needs to stop, outsourced, on hold)*:	Budget is more than $$. What are the resources you need to be successful? Think broadly and take into account your Stakeholder community.
4	Current State *(specific, measurable for clarity)*:	Clearly define what you have now (not everyone is aware), use metrics where possible
5	Level of Change - *(Incremental, Developmental, Transformational)*:	Be clear on the level of change, incremental is easier, transformational takes longer and means lots of loss, developmental is in the middle.
6	Desired State *(Vision & S.M.A.R.T. Goals)*:	Specific, inspiring, clear and aligned to your Higher Purpose, Core Values and Stakeholder Needs
7	Rationale for the Change *(why, hard / soft savings, alignment to YES!)*:	Rock solid rationale. Test a few times before going public. Get feedback and really listen. People must be able to easily repeat this message.
8	Stakeholders Impacted:	Clearly define who this impacts, the real ripple effect can be huge.
9	Stakeholder Needs *(now & after the change)*:	Clearly define the Stakeholder Needs now and after the change is implemented and how this change is beneficial.
10	Others Who May Need to Know & Why *(and when they should be told)*:	Make it clear how long the story needs to stay inside. People want to talk. Give them specifics and a clear 'why' to appeal to head and heart.
11	Losses by those affected *(refer to DISC Styles, Shadow Fears)*:	Loss during change is real. Identify loss, empathize and give time to heal. Change aligned with Higher Purpose focuses people on what to do vs. what to whine about. Honor the old traditions, they are emotional and real.
12	Change Leadership/Executive Team:	Who in the executive circles do you need? Having a clear message for the above items helps to gain alignment. Get them involved for support.
13	Executive & Investment Support Needed *(Time/Money/Politics)*:	Be ready to clearly ask for support with metrics where possible.
14	Communication Vehicles & Tactics *(make messaging repeatable)*:	How can you get the messaging across to all Stakeholders? T-Shirts, coffee mugs, email, billboards, contests, meetings…
15	Role Modeling - To Do's for leaders	What words and actions do you need from leadership. Be specific. Give them presentations, activities to perform at meetings, pre-written emails…
16	Guiding Team / Thought Leaders – *Actors (Early Adopters, Change Leaders)*:	ID the early adopters (troublemakers) who can help you tell the story about what you are trying to accomplish.
17	Change Implementation Team – *Detailers (Details, Project Mgmt.)*:	Who can pull together the details (rules) to accomplish the day to day work to make this real (they are not the early adopters).
18	Pilot or trial program *(get started, run an experiment)*:	Can you run an experiment, to get something going? Start a pilot to prove the concept? Experiments are learning labs and are safe.
19	Anticipated Obstacles, Restraining Forces *(list from Stakeholder discussions)*:	What will emerge and get in the way? Other people may see this much earlier than you will. Listening carefully to Stakeholders will help uncover future challenges.
20	Success / Adoption Checkpoints & Metrics:	How will people know they are winning? What checkpoints can you build to keep the initiative full of vigor? 90 days max between checkpoints.
21	Team & Individual Goals, Scoring Strategies:	How will each participant and team keep score to know they are winning (critical for engagement and inspiration – best to let each group come up with strategies for keepings score)
22	Tools, Training & Education Required *(account for super-users to luddites)*:	What people need to be successful. Make sure to consider for time and cost to train and implement.
23	Review and Recognition (celebration) Process, Dates *(90 day max)*:	How we will celebrate success and have a post-project debrief. This is best determined by the Stakeholders involved, and is critical for developing wisdom in the organization. Science shows 90 days is the max time between sessions.

This page is for notes

A leader is one who knows the way, goes the way, and shows the way. John C. Maxwell

The following pages expand on each of the tenets of Everyday Practical Leadership. There are ideas, stories and more to help you be successful. The bottom of this page is reference for the leadership strategy that Everyday Practical Leadership supports. That core strategy should always be at the top of your mind as you go forward. Create winners!

The summary of Everyday Practical Leadership is below for reference.

Tenets	Summary of each Tenet
1. Building Enthusiasm	To be inspired or engaged in my work, I have to care about it. This tenet takes you and your team through a safe and motivating process of figuring out your YES; why you care about each other and what you do. Skip this tenet and what your organization does (your YES), for 67% [2] of your employees is just work.
2. Conditions for Victory (CFV)	Everyone must know, empirically what it means to win, or they really don't know how to fully participate or if what they do matters. This tenet gives the power of winning at elements that serve your YES, discovered above, over to your team. Skip this tenet and you will forever be the one coming up with answers (vs. your team inspired to create a better future).
3. Achieving Results	All teams want to know the score. This tenet puts scoring in the hands of the team and helps them to know they are winning. Skip this tenet and you lose A players that want to win, B players that want to learn and you keep C players that you don't want (it becomes a race to the bottom for talent).
4. Enabling Success	The tools and training to do the job are required to win. This tenet takes a unique look at this often 'assumed' process. Skip this tenet and your team is powerless to deliver results.
5. Developing Wisdom	Sharing our learning as a team helps us grow. This tenet supports team growth and learning by use of a safe 'Continuous Improvement' process. Skip this tenet and your will repeat mistakes, never build (or rebuild) a sense of 'team' and be caught in a cycle of slow regression to failure.

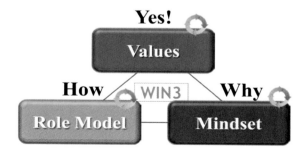

1. Our YES!, what we are excited about (Values)
2. How I show Up (Role Model) impacts everyone
3. My Why (Leadership Mindset) impacts my Yes and my How, I need to be in touch with it and bring it honor

Building Enthusiasm *Tenet #1*

The role of the leader has changed from one of *know the answer* to *coaching the team*. In an uncertain and complicated future, we must build strong teams that will solve the issues, conquer the problems and build real value for our Stakeholder community.

'Never doubt that a small group of thoughtful, committed, organized citizens can change the world; indeed, it's the only thing that ever has.' *Margaret Mead*

Tenets & Guiding Principles	Activities to support the Tenets and Guiding Principles
1. Building Enthusiasm ❖ **Role Models** ❖ **Know Core Stakeholders** ❖ **Stakeholder Needs** ❖ **Higher Purpose** ❖ **Shared Core Values**	1. Agree we are a team, we represent ourselves and each other all the time 2. Map Core Stakeholders as a team (the ones we focus on) 3. Team members meet with Stakeholders and report on Stakeholder Needs[1] 4. Produce a set of Team Core Values[2], what we commit to and stand for 5. Generate a team set of 'Beliefs & Behaviors' to support Core Values 6. Create Team Vision Board – where we are going, values, beliefs, behaviors 7. Team Higher Purpose based on Stakeholder Needs and Core Values

This tenet is about creating an inspired mind-set.

To be inspired or engaged in my work, I have to care about the work. This tenet takes you and your team through a safe and motivating process of figuring out your YES (commonly known as your Higher Purpose), why you care about each other and care about what you do. Skip this tenet and what your organization does (your YES/Higher Purpose), for 67% [2] of your employees is just 'work.'

Without enthusiasm for the work you do, nothing will change. Think about it, everyone is enthusiastic about something. Sometimes people are enthusiastic about how little money they make, or how hard their job is, or how little they are appreciated. Everybody puts energy into something, we might as well help them put the right amount of energy into the right priorities at work and help us all deliver valued added results to our Stakeholder community.

You are the leader, you set the team up for success and part of that setup is building enthusiasm focused on serving Stakeholder Needs and Higher Purpose. You are responsible for making sure that everyone on your team is clearly on the same page as to what they are enthusiastic about. The days are gone where people are enthusiastic about their paycheck (pay is important, but its not the driver it was in previous years). People want purpose, they want growth and learning. Tenet number one and the guiding principles help you build Stakeholder focused enthusiasm.

Enthusiasm on a team grows from a number of facets. EPL uses a mix of internal and external aspects to enable you to build enthusiasm. We will get to team enthusiasm in a moment, first though, you (the leader) have to get started!

There is one thing though that is not on the list above. Its this – you as the leader, have to decide you are going to let go of the old command-and-control paradigm and begin to coach your team towards success. Think of it this way, stop telling and start leading. The real first activity is for you to set up a meeting with your team and to let them know that you have decided to adopt a new model. A model that engages the best of all of them together, building purpose, service to Stakeholders, learning and success into the everyday life of the team. At this meeting you will have a kickoff

Notes:

"I reminded myself everyday, I am a role model." Bill Gooding

and introduce the Everyday Practical Leadership model with simple straightforward activities to help the team become engaged.

If you are not sure how to write the introductory speech, you can use the following to get started:

'I have called you here today, because our world is changing. I also know that the power and goodness of this team holds incredible promise for our future, and we need to tap into it. I believe in this team enough to make a change for the better for all of us. It is simply this, adopting a new approach to what it is we do. None of us can participate in this alone, only all of us can. It's not hard, it's fun, and as we embark on this new way of operating, it will be up to this team to create our future. We are going to tap into the power of our purpose and to serving the needs of our Stakeholder community. The first step is that we need to determine who our core Stakeholders are, what they need, what they expect from us and how we serve them.'

You can probably write words to get your team excited better than we can. Use the planning pages to get started.

Role modeling is an interesting concept that makes a lot of sense to people once they think about it. The crux of the situation is this; people on a team, need to understand that they represent the team and the organization in everything they do and say. This includes conversations with each other and with Stakeholders. Some people do not understand how important they are to the organization and to the people around them.

How you help people on your team understand the importance of role modeling is up to you. However, you have to be a role model first. And that basically comes down to asking this question, 'Would I want to be a person having a conversation or interactions with me all the time?'

How you treat your people and come across to your people is how they will treat each other and your Stakeholder community. You have to set an example (actually, you are always setting an example, just remember to make sure it is the right one.). There are many ways to gain feedback on how you are coming across such as a 360 survey, asking people for feedback and hiring a coach to help you through the process.

The activities in appendix 1 and 2 are specifically designed to help you step through the process of discovering and building your teams prioritized Core Values and Higher Purpose. Once accomplished, you can move on to tenet number two. However if you skip the tenets of developing Core Values and Higher Purpose your team will be focused on fixing their own internal problems versus creating solutions for your Stakeholders.

Do not skip the tenets in building enthusiasm, because enthusiasm gets into the heart and becomes a driver when the going gets tough. Creating a team Vision Board can be a very enlightening experience for a team. Google 'Vision Boards' and you'll see ideas. There is no one right way to do them, however the wrong way is to not do them at all.

Notes:

[2] Reference Gallup State of the American Workplace study, 2017

Defining the Conditions for Victory *Tenet #2*

The problem with most goals is many teams don't feel like they own them or understand them. It is time to change that problem.

'Inspiration only comes from the idea that you can make a difference. In the end, inspiration requires and depends on an emotional commitment.' Brue Wayne McClellan, Spiritual Coach

2. Conditions for Victory (CFV)	
❖ **Team Built Goals** ❖ **Stakeholder & Higher Purpose Focused** ❖ **S.M.A.R.T. Goals**	1. Team creates a S.M.A.R.T. Goal based on Stakeholder Needs honoring Higher Purpose, Core Values and Beliefs 2. Goal time should be 2 – 4 weeks out, no longer 3. Set the date for #5 – Developing Wisdom (and how you will celebrate) 4. Goal must have everyone involved – no one person/few can carry the team • S.M.A.R.T. - *Simple | Measurable | Attainable | Realistic | Time-Bound (see Appendix 5 for more details)*

This tenet is about developing goals your team will buy into and really:

- Understand
- Support
- Be enthusiastic about achieving

This tenet also helps your team to support their Core Values and Higher Purpose. And, just as importantly, the processes in this tenet develop the team's intrinsic motivation. (Note: intrinsic motivation is something that drives me from inside versus extrinsic motivation something external that drives me. An example of intrinsic motivation might be my personal Higher Purpose and extrinsic motivation is my paycheck). Intrinsic is stronger, more powerful and will weather a storm.

On another note, having predictable and understandable goals is important to the psychology of the team. In the research report book, 'The Craving Mind,' Judson Brewer reports that brain scans of depressed people and people without goals turned up pretty much the same.[1]

It is time to get your team focused on the right activities. You may have been like most managers and been coming up with what things your team should be doing and when. You need to stop that. Let them set goals if you really want them engaged.

Here's the question to ask your team, "What do we need to do to be more successful in honoring our Core Values and Higher Purpose?" If your team has never been part of goal setting, you may get blank stares. If this is the case, put out a couple of ideas. However it is important that the team does not continue to use your ideas, you want them to come up with their own ideas – then they own them.

Most of my clients at this point say, 'Wait a minute, we have company metrics that we have to adhere to.' You must still adhere to all of your company metrics. The big question is, what are the activities that your team can undertake to improve their output so that in the end your company metrics and goals are met?

You as the leader look at the larger picture and all the interconnecting processes. Your team will probably focus on what they can control. Let them find ways to improve, and they will improve how they operate on a regular basis. Don't ask them to fix the whole problem, they need to fix their parts where they have control and influence.

Notes:

_____

_____

_____

_____

_____

_____

_____

_____

_____

_____

_____

_____

_____

_____

_____

[1] The Craving Mind, Yale University Press, ISBN-13: 978-0300234367

"Don't worry about winning or losing, if you want to grow your team and your business, just look at new opportunities as running an experiment." Richard Sheridan, CEO Menlo Innovations

> *Here is a simple example with a surprising payoff:*
>
> *In one of our client's factories, reducing cost and waste were big issues. Once a manager <u>asked</u> their team what ideas <u>they</u> had about reducing cost and waste, the team came up with a way to recycle specialty bags they used in their manufacturing operation. In the end after a pilot experiment, the team ended up saving $24,000 a year in bags (true story).*

Let's explore goal setting. The first thing about setting goals is that your team may not be skilled at setting good goals. That is expected, you may have to go through a period of setting some goals that may be a little odd. The exercise of goal setting sometimes is to learn how to set goals. The key point to remember is that goals that are set by your team will be embraced by your team.

The second part of this is that goals must be S.M.A.R.T in order to be successful. The appendix outlines S.M.A.R.T goals and also includes a page of exercises where you can look at goals and see how S.M.A.R.T they really are.

Remember the secret sauce – you need to let the team set their own goals (yes, continue to honor company metrics). The cycle time for these goals should only be 2-4 weeks. These are smaller goals that the team can concentrate on, feel like winners and see progress.

Look at it this way, if your team cycles through one new goal a month and learns from it then by the end of the year you have increased the effectiveness of the team by an incredible amount.

A special caveat needs to be mentioned though. We have experienced teams that get so excited about owning their own goals, that they shoot for the moon. A S.M.A.R.T goal is attainable, make sure the goal the team agrees to is realistic and achievable.

Make sure that when the goals are set, everyone on the team is included in the goal. This is not a time for a star player, is it time for everyone to work together. As an example, we had one team commit to five Stakeholder interviews over a two-week period for each person. You could do more, however no one could do less. If anyone on the team had less than five interviews, the team failed. It was amazing to watch them help each other achieve their goal.

At this point make sure you set a date for tenet #5 - Developing Wisdom. Tenet #5 should include a celebration when the goal is met. If the goal is not met, still have the meeting to develop wisdom, however there is no celebration. It's as simple and cut and dry as that. However, when people work hard for something they want to celebrate when they win. Actually, they <u>need</u> to celebrate when they win – or they get deflated and tired, disengaged and uninspired.

Think of it this way, at the end of the World Series, champagne bottles being opened in the locker room for the winning team. And that's the way we need to do it in business.

Achieving Results *Tenet #3*

Winning matters to everyone. But they have to know and understand the score. The other part is, when they help keep score, they are totally involved.

FAIL = First Attempt at Learning Cheryl Adas, Conscious Leader facilitator, designer and champion of doing what is right

3. Achieving Results ❖ **Team Developed Scoring & Updating** ❖ **Visual and Public** ❖ **Only Team Can Win**	1. Team determines how to score the Conditions for Victory and team members do the scorekeeping (not the leader) 2. Tracking must be visual and public on how each team member and the team are tracking toward CFV 3. Only the team wins, no person or group carries the team

Notes:

This tenet is really about keeping score and enabling your team to know they are winning (or losing) on a visceral and emotional level and be engaged in the process (in terms and a format that matters to them). This is where you track the goal that you set in tenet #2.

Lets face it, most of the metrics in companies are heard as *blah blah blah* by the lion's share of employees. Its noise and means nothing but 'more work for me.'

This tenet is actually fairly easy to achieve, and keeps the process interesting.

Here is how it works. In the previous tenet, the team set a goal. It should be a good S.M.A.R.T goal. Now you ask the team how they want to keep score. And when they figure out how <u>they</u> want to keep score, you let the team do the scorekeeping. The goal turns into their 'game.' Its their goal, its their scoreboard, its their game.

You will probably continue to do the scorekeeping for your company metrics. That is understandable and perfectly acceptable. However for the shorter team goal, it is important from a buy-in engagement, to let the team keep score. And they can be as creative as they want in their scorekeeping (see examples on the next page).

> The story of Mike and how <u>not</u> to keep score:
>
> One of my clients (Mike) had always loved keeping score of everything in his operation. He was very good at it and had set up a number of automated processes to gather data from complex systems. Every month he published a graphical scorecard that included millions of data points about the operation. I tried in vain to have him enable his very capable teams to set up small goals for each of their respective functions. Mike would have nothing of it. He felt that the tracking he did was enough, however in the same breath Mike would complain that projects were not completed on time nor were they tracked well in his system. He also talked about the fact that he never got feedback from his published scorecards. The data he tracked was important to his management, but not to his teams and they were very frustrated. Mike and his teams continue to struggle to this day.
>
> A facsimile example of Mike's monthly charts appears on the next page at the bottom. It has a red X at the top to remind you to not do this.

"Nothing great was ever achieved without enthusiasm." Ralph Waldo Emerson

The story of another Mike and how to keep score.

This Mike was different, he was struggling with his maintenance team to keep up with machinery that got very dirty and very expensive to run when it got dirty. However his team did not seem interested anymore in achieving their weekly results.

Mike set up EPL by the book, and within a month every machine was up to spec and the team was even doing extra work because now they were proud of what they were doing. Plant tours now included their equipment and Mike's team participated in these tours.

The long story is this, failure to maintain that equipment could result in failure to the tune of millions of dollars. Now Mike's team is not only saving the company operational costs, they are saving an extreme level of capital investment.

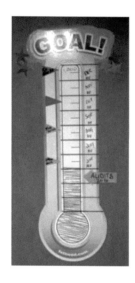

Scorekeeping by teams is generally not complicated. And it can be fun. The thermometer to the right is used in a customer service call center. The team routinely tracks their goals on the thermometer and at the end of each week erases the thermometer and starts over. The manager of the call center says that it's incredible, the power of the visual on the wall because the people on her team know that they are winning or losing on a constant basis.

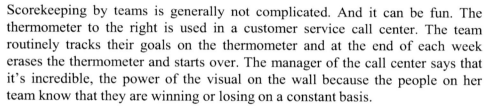

The scorecard in the center of the page represents a team committed to having Stakeholder conversations. Every time a Stakeholder conversation took place, a team member put a mark on the chart. You can see there are a couple of overachievers, however the goal was that everyone on the team had five discussions and that was the only way to win. An interesting note is, on the last day of the project one of the team members was short one interview, and another team member helped him out to make sure that the team won (positive peer-pressure at work).

The last chart is a facsimile from our friend Mike and his story on the previous page. Every data point was important to the organization, however those data points really meant nothing to the feet on the street that were supporting the operation. It's really about letting go of control, or the illusion of control. Giving control over to the team on what's really important to them, especially once they have established an understanding of what Stakeholder needs are, is very inspiring.

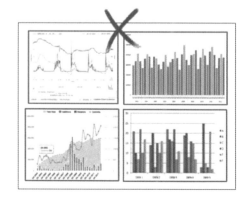

As you can imagine, when the team keeps score and everyone has to participate then peer pressure becomes very intense. It's important that the scoring be out in public where the team and Stakeholders are able to see it on a regular basis. Just like a professional sports game, we don't want to hide the score.

Enabling Success *Tenet #4*

I have to be empowered to win, and that includes having the tools, knowledge and policy support of the organization. If I can't win, I am helpless and not inspired.

The word SILENT contains the same letters as the words LISTEN

4. Enabling Success ❖ **Supportive Practices & Policies** ❖ **Actionable Tools** ❖ **Education**	1. Leader must ensure that organizational practices, policy, and procedures are supportive of the Conditions for Victory 2. The Team requests tools and education necessary to meet the CFV 3. Leader searches for tools and education to enable victory – ask the questions, 'What do we need for victory? What is in our way?' 4. Training comes from inside expertise as often as possible 5. Remind team of the date for #5 – Developing Wisdom

Notes:

This tenet is about helping your team win as well as utilizing an often missed, incredibly valuable and under developed resource (and its almost free).

Often we assume that people know how to get things accomplished and they have all the tools they need to complete the job. However a Gallup poll showed that many people do not have the tools they need to complete their job (http://news.gallup.com/topic/element_2_materials_and_equipment.aspx).

As the leader it is your job to listen to what is in people's way and remove those obstacles and barriers. Sometimes it is simple training and tools, sometimes it is systems and policies. The insidious thing about these kinds of problems is that sometimes employees don't even understand what is in their own way.

One of the secrets to success that we have found over the years also is using your internal best resources. Here is what we mean by that. Generally on the team there is someone or some people who are doing a great job. Instead of hiring outside help why not utilize those people to show others how they get to be so successful!

When you utilize these people to show others how to win, a number of things happen. First of all you are using someone to do training who understands the nuances of your operation.

Secondly, there is a certain conscious and/or unconscious pride that emerges from the team when the team is able to learn from themselves.

And finally, the people who are doing the training feel really great! Imagine the conversation when someone goes home from work and says the team picked me to do some training because I do such a great job. We have seen people experience this, and they just could never believe that they could be in a position to help others and to be so important.

It is vital that you help the people who are going to do the training to learn how to train. There is nothing more frustrating from either the teacher or the learner side of having to work with someone who is not prepared to be successful in a training environment. The following page contains some tips and tricks for developing a training program that you can share with the team.

The Quick Start Training Planner

Notes:

Developing training (it is often wise to engage a training developer to help your subject matter experts put together a great training program. Sometimes that is not practical and the following tips can be used to put together a program):

1. **Develop Objectives**

   The best training programs have clear measurable objectives and planned outcomes, and the easiest way to develop an objective is to complete the following sentence (you might have multiple objectives) – "When the participant has completed this training they will be able to…"

2. **Test the Objectives**

   Run your objectives by your target audience. Ask them for feedback, input and ideas. They may come up with ideas that you may have missed. Also though, more importantly, when it comes time to the training they will have some ownership in it and they will be much more interested in fully participating.

3. **Plan Many Exercises**

   Statistically, at least 75% of the population learns best by doing things. It is wise to plan many hands-on exercises for people to test their knowledge and become comfortable with the learning.

4. **Test your program and be prepared to modify the training**

   Many training programs are well-designed, however, when it gets into the rollout stage it is obvious that some things need to change. Plan for that and don't be surprised when it happens. It even happens to some of the best trainers and developers (note – it always happens). The best approach to training sometimes is knowing that you are running an experiment and you will have to modify things as you learn and grow smarter.

5. **Solicit feedback after the training**

   Written and verbal feedback can be invaluable for your team. It also tells them that you are listening to what is important to them. Feedback is important to the trainers and also to the participants. People naturally want to have input into a training program that they are participating in.

6. **Celebrate**

   Training is hard work. It is good to celebrate after successful training initiative, and let people know that the energy they put into the program mattered. Certificates of completion are always a good idea and are easy to create.

Developing Wisdom *Tenet #5*

If we work hard and win, we must celebrate and learn from our efforts. There is so much we can learn from each other, if we invest the time. We need to invest in ourselves!

'The only organizations to survive in this turbulent world are learning organizations.' Peter Senge, 5th Discipline

5. Developing Wisdom	
❖ Review ❖ Celebration ❖ Learning	1. Before the session, remind team members to bring thoughts around R/W/D/H or C/S/S/H to the session in writing. 2. Invite Stakeholders to be involved in these sessions whenever possible 3. Use the Parking Lot with Post-Its during the session (stay on target) 4. Run the review session using R/W/D/H (Right/Wrong/Different/How) or C/S/S/H (Continue/Stop/Start/How[3]) 5. Celebration only occurs when the team goal(s) is achieved – we honor effort and celebrate success

Notes:

This tenet is about so many things:

- Building up the spirit and energy of your team
- Creating a learning environment where it is safe to get better together
- Supporting each other in knowledge and wisdom
- Helping you (the leader) understand where the team is at, and where they are heading
- Creating long-term excitement, buy-in and a Can-Do attitude

And this tenet, among all the other tenets is so often missed and when its missed it tears people up, disenfranchises them, and is almost cruel. Here is why.

Your people show up and work hard (that is their perception and you know that is true). But, what do they most often hear about? Problems that they have to fix and goals the company has for blah blah blah.

A piece of the problem is that we often focus on the 'problem' and not on the solution or the people who we expect to fix the issues, nor do we spend any time celebrating our successes or sharing our learning. And basically people get deflated over time. They fundamentally just get tired. We have to pump them up, and really pump them. Emotionally, physically, publicly and spiritually. We are not machines. We desire to learn, grow, be successful and achieve goals. As leaders, we have to feed those innate desires for our team to grow. If we don't, we have not created a balanced learning environment, and people will check out – the good ones leave, and the mediocre stay. You begin to participate in a race to the bottom for talent, energy and enthusiasm.

This tenet builds people up and it's not hard. You will have set the date for this event a while back (ideally during tenet #2). It may take a couple of cycles of goal setting, keeping score and developing wisdom before people get the hang of the cycle. That is okay, you are building a learning organization.

A couple of days before the session, remind people that you are going to have the session and they should bring a list of things that went well, did not go well, should be different and ideas on how to get there (this is the Right/Wrong/Different/How model – often abbreviated as R/W/D/H).

Often the celebration includes food, sometimes it includes some sort of prize. It is best to have the R/W/D/H discussion before diving into the food. However, use your best.

"You get what you celebrate." Dean Kamen, inventor of the Segway

A sad story, with a happy ending:

I was the training liaison to a product development project a while back. We invested $32M in a new platform product and spent 3 years launching it worldwide with great success (the product dominated its market for 10 years). After the last rollout session in the last country, I called a meeting with the team and we had a 'Wisdom' session. It went well. We related stories of R/W/D from all corners of the globe. We shared our triumphs and tragedies before the team disbanded to pursue other projects.

After the meeting, the product manager pulled me aside and commented about how incredibly powerful that experience was. He told me they had never done a postmortem meeting before.

I later reflected on his comments and it occurred to me why the previous three rollouts that I had been involved with from a field perspective had shared some of the same issues.

The good news, the design team began working on a new platform which a few years later took a new market with new technology by storm. And interestingly enough, none of the old issues emerged.

Notes:

judgment. If cocktails are present, all serious business discussion is over (remember, you are all still role models).

We have found it to be a very powerful thing to have Stakeholders present at these discussions. People tend to be on their best behavior and Stakeholders lend a reference to objective thought that your team members find difficult or impossible. The external reference is a very powerful influence!

Now a word on the Parking Lot. Have Post-It Notes® available for the team (or a checkbox available if the meeting is digital). When something occurs to someone that is important however possibly not important to this session, have them write their thought on a Post-it note and put it on the Parking Lot. This way they feel heard, they get the thought off their chest, and if it's a good idea, is saved for later.

Finally, lets talk about whether or not the celebration occurs. We often hear, "We got close, so we had the party." WRONG. The team has to achieve the goal to celebrate. You must make sure the goal is achievable (not too high, not too low). It is demeaning to the team to have a celebration for a goal that was realistic and then not met. The subtle message to the group is, 'You don't really need to work hard and try.' And the message to the people working hard is, 'You got suckered.'

When the team wins together, learns together and celebrates together (including Stakeholders), bonds form that build the team into a cohesive force that ~~can~~ will conquer any challenge they face.

[1] http://infed.org/mobi/peter-senge-and-the-learning-organization/

This page is for notes

Appendices for Everyday Practical Leadership

Appendix

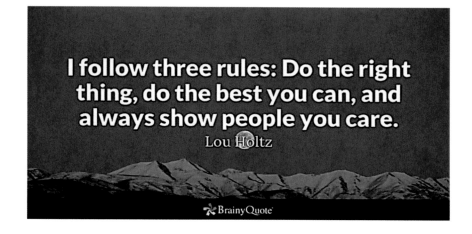

This page is for notes

Our Core Values are foundational primary guiding principles often dictating our behavior, action/re-action and are a main filter for our response in any given situation (individually we may have many Core Values, both personal and professional).

Core Values help us to know and determine what is 'right from wrong' (and defines our perspective on things). From a corporate sense, Core Values can help companies determine if they are on the right path and fulfilling their business goals (Higher Purpose). When we become aware of and purposeful of our Core Values, this can help us create an unwavering and unchanging guide to running our business and our life.

Core Values…
1. Can govern personal relationships
2. Create our perceptions of other people and situations
3. Guide our processes and actions
4. Help clarify who we are
5. Articulate to others (and our self) what we stand for
6. Guide us in making decisions
7. Require no external justification

Core Values are not…
1. Operating practices (they guide the practices)
2. Business strategies (they influence strategies)
3. Cultural norms (they do help develop and influence cultural norms)
4. Competencies (they may guide us in what we pay attention to and develop in ourselves)
5. Changed in response to day to day changes in life (transformations however may change Core Values)

Clarity in Core Values
Being clear on Core Values is critical for leading others. Great leaders share Core Values and live them in every interaction. Great leaders inspect their Core Values with an objective view and often alter or morph a perspective on a Core Value as they grow. As they mature, great leaders question the validity of the perspective of their Core Values and purposefully determine their path based on purpose driven by Core Values.

In any relationship, when our Core Values are violated, it is through our integrity that we maintain good behavior to stand up for what is right vs what is easy. Its simply developing the ability to respond well.

Determining Core Values and order of importance:
1. Select 10 Core Values from the next page or create your own (more ideas at www.OurThreads.com)
2. Write these Core Values on the top of the **Core Values Prioritization** page.
3. Rank the 10 Core Values you chose using the process on the worksheet.
4. Write them in the top 5 box.
5. You may create a Wordle of your Core Values at: http://www.wordle.net/create The heading at the top of this page was created at wordle.net. One client created a screen saver from their team's Core Values – see below on creating team Core Values. Note: must use a browser that supports JAVA (Chrome does not support JAVA).

Clarifying your team's Core Values 'friction gap'
Often on a team, there seems to be friction. Frequently that friction comes from a three-way disparity. The disparity arises from a difference between each team member's personal Core Values, existing perceived Core Values of the team and what each team member wants the Core Values of the team to be. Think of this as a Core Values 'friction gap.'

There is a fairly simple exercise you may undertake to help the team understand:
1. The importance of Core Values
2. How very different each team member's personal Core Values might be
3. How each team member views the team now
4. How each team member would like the team to operate

The best thing for you to do right now to go through the personal Core Values exercise on the next 2 pages to understand how it operates. Then you can take your team through the steps outlined in the Team Core Values exercise page (spare Prioritization Worksheets are provided later in this book).

Communication Tip – when you meet with your team and determine Core Values, record them and share them. Celebrate them. And, through experience, this exercise for some people is a very powerful awakening. Respecting this process is <u>very</u> important.

Sample List of Core Values

The list of values below is used by the Barrett Values Centre®. The Barrett Values Center works tirelessly helping organizations put values at the heart of how people live and work. We thank them for allowing us to use their list of values to help you begin your journey into a values driven life.

The link at the bottom of the page takes you to the **Barrett Personal Values Assessment (PVA)** should you want to experience that (its free and its enlightening). The PVA is a great exercise in looking at your Core Values and what they mean. Should you need it, a longer list of values ideas may be found at www.OurThreads.com.

Pick 10 of the values below and write them at the top of the next page, or use your own (in no particular order).

- accountability
- achievement
- adaptability
- ambition
- balance (home/work)
- being liked
- being the best
- caring
- caution
- clarity
- coaching/ mentoring
- commitment
- community involvement
- compassion
- competence
- conflict resolution
- continuous learning
- control
- courage
- creativity
- dialogue
- ease with uncertainty
- efficiency
- enthusiasm/ positive attitude
- entrepreneurial
- environmental awareness
- ethics
- excellence
- fairness
- family
- financial stability
- forgiveness
- friendship
- future generations

- generosity
- health
- humility
- humor/ fun
- independence
- initiative
- integrity
- job security
- leadership
- listening
- making a difference
- openness
- patience
- perseverance
- personal fulfilment
- personal growth
- personal image
- power
- professional growth
- recognition
- reliability
- respect
- reward
- risk-taking
- safety
- self-discipline
- teamwork
- trust
- vision
- wealth
- well-being (physical/ emotional/ mental/ spiritual)
- wisdom

Barrett Values Centre Personal Values Assessment:
https://www.valuescentre.com/our-products/products-individuals/personal-values-assessment-pva

Core Values Prioritization Worksheet

Step 1: List your **top 10** Core Values (don't worry about putting them in a priority order yet)

a. _____   f. _____

b. _____   g. _____

c. _____   h. _____

d. _____   i. _____

e. _____   j. _____

Step 2: Compare your values to each other in groups of two, circle the highest priority in each of the two match-ups below:

a	a	a	a	a	a	a	a	a
b	c	d	e	f	g	h	i	j

b	b	b	b	b	b	b	b
c	d	e	f	g	h	i	j

c	c	c	c	c	c	c
d	e	f	g	h	i	j

d	d	d	d	d	d
e	f	g	h	i	j

e	e	e	e	e
f	g	h	i	j

f	f	f	f
g	h	i	j

g	g	g
h	i	j

h	h
i	j

i
j

My Top 5 Core Values:

1. _____

2. _____

3. _____

4. _____

5. _____

You may create a Wordle at:
http://www.wordle.net/create
Note: must use a browser that supports JAVA
(Chrome does not support JAVA)

Count up # of "wins" for each:

a____   b____   c____   d____   e____   f____   g____   h____   i____   j____

The top values by vote (insert letters here, circle the priorities at the top of the page, add to **My Top 5 Core Values**):

#1 _____   #2 _____   #3 _____   #4 _____   #5 _____

Adapted from Appendix E, "Where Do I Go With My Life?" by Crystal & Bolles

Team Core Values, Stakeholder Needs & Higher Purpose Process

These exercises and process helps the team understand each other and focus on valid priorities.[1]

In this exercise, we work to understand the importance of our individual Core Values, our current team Core Values, what is important to our Stakeholders and our expected team Core Values. Honoring and understanding differences/similarities between these helps us understand why things might or might not work as we strive together to serve our Higher Purpose (this process can take a few weeks or longer. Its worth it and leads to inspiring your team).

The process is fairly simple, follow these steps (Tip – when you have team meetings, record outcomes and share with the team. It tells them that this process matters). Approach all sessions with an attitude of curiosity.

1. **My Core Values**

2. **My Perception of the Team's Current Core Values**

3. **Understanding and Sharing Stakeholder Needs**

4. **My Perception of the Team's Future Core Values**

5. **Agreeing on the Team's Future Core Values**

6. **Developing the Team's Higher Purpose**

1. My Core Values

1. Make at least 3 copies of the Core Values Prioritization Worksheet for each member of the team (some people go through the process a couple of times, we have had many people share the process with friends and family).

2. Each person on the team completes the Core Values Prioritization Worksheet for themselves. This is done as an individual exercise; the process can take a few minutes for some, and much longer for others. It does not work well in a group setting because some people may need considerable time to effectively complete the exercise.

   Before people leave to develop their prioritized Core Values, as the leader you should share your Core Values so people can see the outcome and how the next session will unfold. This helps people see how it is done and prepares them mentally, emotionally and visually for the experience. We have seen leaders share a simple list, colorful posters or a Wordle (http://www.wordle.net). Your team will appreciate you (the leader) setting them up for success and being a good role model.

3. In a later group session, each person shares their list of Core Values. In the ensuing discussion, explore with curiosity the differences and similarities. No-one's Core Values can be labeled as 'wrong.' Talk about how knowing and understanding our Core Values helps us to work together (Simply this: when I know you, I can understand you better, respect you, and how you operate).

2. My Perception of the Team's Current Core Values

1. Each person on the team completes the Core Values Prioritization Worksheet indicating their view of the team's current Core Values (from their perspective).

2. At a meeting (with knowledge before hand), each team member shares their Core Values list on their perception of the team's current Core Values. No-one's perception of current Core Values can be labeled as 'wrong.'

3. In a group discussion, explore the perceived Core Values differences and similarities. Agree as a team that we should have one set of prioritized Core Values that we know, respect and for which we hold ourselves accountable.

4. Do not create a set of Core Values for the team at this time. Go the next step.

---

[1]. This process is a combination of seminal principles emanating from research and experiences of Gallup's multiple State of the American Workplace reports, The Barrett Values Centre (UK), Sparks and Associates Group Culture, Firms of Endearment, and Kotter's Corporate Culture & Performance.

3. Understanding and Sharing Stakeholder Needs

This next step provides focus for team members around what is critical.

First, map your core Stakeholders. The easiest way is to draw a circle and then ask the question, 'Who are our internal and external Stakeholders?' These are the people you touch, the people who would miss you if you went away. These are the people where you drive value. Sometimes these discussions get deep, because a team never realized how many people they impacted *(we once worked with a packaging company and their teams had never thought about Stakeholders from the perspective of the manufacturer right down to the babies and mothers who used the products that came in the packaging our client produced. It was an eye-opener and motivator for a lot of teams in that factory).*

Using the guidelines laid out on the pages titled **Stakeholder Discussions – Guidelines** have all team members participate in discussions with Stakeholders. It is best to have the team decide who they will speak with and a reasonable deadline for having the discussions. Usually a deadline of between two and four weeks works best. Remember, Stakeholders include anyone (or company/group) that you have an impact on. Stakeholders can be internal and external to the organization. You should have a good mix of both internal and external Stakeholders that you speak with.

After a few Stakeholder discussions have taken place, have the team discuss what they heard from the Stakeholders. Generally what happens, is that after a few rounds of these discussions, themes begin to emerge.

It is important to take good notes during these discussions. Writing information on flipcharts or recording it via a PC and projector help people to see, understand and connect with the themes that are emerging. These Stakeholder stories might go on for a few sessions, and after a few stories are told, people who were hesitant to go through the process generally get on board.

4. My Perception of the Team's Future Core Values

Using the **Core Values Prioritization Worksheet**, have each team member create their expectations of what the team's Core Values should be in the future. Have team members share their list during a meeting. Take time to understand the similarities and the differences from different team members.

Remember, at this point team members will now be talking from a perception of what Stakeholders need versus only an internal perception of what has been going on. Having a Stakeholder view when developing Core Values is a critical component to developing a set of Core Values that really matter.

5. Agreeing on the Team's Future Core Values

This next exercise is a good team building experience. As a group, aggregate the list from the step above and go through the prioritization process as a team to come up with the team's future Core Values.

We have had leaders create posters from this list of Core Values, a wordle (http://www.wordle.net) that then becomes a screensaver or poster, or team members create a poster of their Core Values.

Once you have a list, let it settle for a while. You might revisit it after a period of time to make sure the list of team Core Values still works.

At this point, you have two options:

1. Continue on to the step below and develop your Higher Purpose or,

2. Exercise Tenet #2 of Everyday Practical Leadership and have the team begin to create goals to help them live and honor their Core Values. If you develop your Higher Purpose first, then goals are set to support your Higher Purpose.

Either choice is fine, however by the time a team gets to their future Core Values, they might be ready for some hands-on work and have had enough of the word exercises for a while. You will know what's best, you know your team.

6. Developing the Team's Higher Purpose

Using the information that you gained from Stakeholder discussions, decide on themes and messaging from your Stakeholders. These discussions can be quite vigorous as people will have different experiences and may have very different perspectives of what is important. Remember, vigorous discussion is very healthy for a group.

You might want to use brainstorming techniques such as agreeing that no ideas are bad. Using Post-it notes to vote on ideas and so forth. The format for your Higher Purpose statement is well described in the book **Find Your Why**[1] (however, the authors leave out the Stakeholder discussion part, and this creates a Higher Purpose that only comes from the inside of the organization. We find that becomes a very unhealthy experience for a team.). Understanding the importance and impact of your Higher Purpose is well described in the publication **Conscious Capitalism: Liberating the Heroic Spirit of Business**[2]. Research supporting the business case for developing and living to your team's Higher Purpose comes from **Firms of Endearment: How World-Class Companies Profit from Passion and Purpose**[3].

A list of organizations and their Higher Purpose appears in the table below. Sometimes seeing these examples helps people to understand the concept of a Higher Purpose.

Organization	Higher Purpose
Zappos:	Delivering Happiness
Ikea:	'People and Planet Positive'
Container Store:	Organization with Heart, 'Get Organized, Be Happy'
Southwest Airlines:	We exist to connect people to what's important in their lives through friendly, reliable, and low-cost air travel.
Patagonia:	Preserving the environment, sustainability in clothing
Crayola:	Helping parents and teachers raise inspired, creative children
Whole Foods Market:	Educating about organic, natural foods and nutritional health

The suggested format for your Higher Purpose statement is basically this:

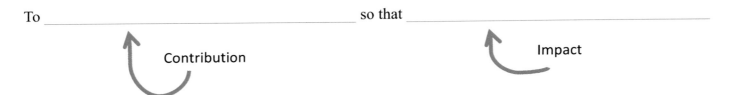

To _____ so that _____

      Contribution   Impact

You can use whatever format you like, the above suggested format seems to work for people, especially when they are getting started.

Once you have a Higher Purpose, have your team put it in a visual format and then tested with Stakeholders. Make sure you thank Stakeholders for their input and ideas in helping you to develop your Higher Purpose.

Your next step is to now engage Tenet #2 in Everyday Practical Leadership, defining the conditions for victory.

---

[1] Find Your Why, published by Portfolio, 9/17. ISBN: 978-0143111726

[2] Conscious Capitalism: Liberating the Heroic Spirit of Business, published by Harvard Business Review Press, 1/14. ISBN: 978-1625271754

[3] Firms of Endearment: How World-Class Companies Profit from Passion and Purpose, published by Pearson FT Press; 2 ed, 2/14. ISBN: 978-0133382594

Stakeholder Discussions - Guidelines

The following guidelines have worked well with our clients. Obviously change things as necessary. One critical component is that you and your team approach this project with curiosity. You may also find the information that you gather so compelling, that you continue on with this process on a regular basis.

1. Introduction to Stakeholder Discussions

As we work to develop our team with strategic and tactical plans, a critical point of reference is to understand implicitly the needs of the various internal and external Stakeholders we serve. As we capture these needs, as a team, the outcomes of these conversations will help us develop and understand our true Higher Purpose and the value we bring to our Stakeholder community.

The guidelines below help you engage in fruitful Stakeholder discussions. These conversations are intended to be exploratory, friendly and enlightening, building greater understanding as well as deeper relationships.

To better understand the concepts supporting Stakeholder discussions, please watch the following overview video about Conscious Capitalism and the tenets of a Conscious Business: https://youtu.be/wp8MCJp5-iM

2. Stakeholder Conversation Guidelines:

These conversations work best with simplicity and transparency (if the focus on your team are nervous about having these discussions, sometimes having a practice session works out well). Many groups find having two members of a team engaged in these conversations as useful (the conversations gather more data).

1. Set the Stakeholder up for success by giving them time to prepare for a fruitful discussion (This may be accomplished via phone call or if needed, email. Using both phone and email is effective).

2. Consider this introduction: "We are working to better understand the needs of our Stakeholders. An element of this effort is the development of a Stakeholder-based organizational Higher Purpose, why we exist. We are now in the phase of gathering feedback from our core Stakeholders. Your answers to three (3) questions will help clarify and validate the true value we bring to (insert company name). The three (3) questions are:

   a. What's going well in regard to your relationship with (insert company name)?

   b. What's not going well in regard to your relationship with (insert company name)?

   c. What needs to be different related to the products and services or relationship we have with you? In other words, what do you need from us to be / feel more successful?"

   d. "Please think these over and can we set 30-60 minutes aside to talk over your feedback in-person on (date & time)?" "I'll send you a meeting notice with the questions. And, I greatly appreciate your help and welcome your candor."

3. Important Tips for Success

1. It is best to give the Stakeholder time to think about answers. Your discussion is best face-to-face. A phone or a video call works if absolutely necessary. Stay conscious of tone and body language. Avoid an email discussion; this data gathering is most successful using an interactive approach (DO NOT do this via on-line survey!).

2. Ideally, two team/company representatives should attend the conversation as a sign of significance and for clarifying understanding (2 sets of ears).

3. The Stakeholder's answer cannot be wrong. **This is critically important.** You may ask clarifying questions, request examples and so forth, but never defend the company or imply the Stakeholder's response is invalid (because it is their point of view).

4. Please remember to thank the Stakeholder for their time, authentic feedback and for helping to make us a better organization and service provider. A follow-up "thank you", email or written note is best practice.

See the next page for tips on data gathering and structure.

4. Data Gathering and Repository

After each discussion, please capture your conversation via a structured method. This will lend consistency to the stories and enables themes to more easily emerge. The following data labels work well (you can set up a free survey at www.surveymonkey.com):

1. Interviewer Names (your team members) – usually two people at each session

2. Stakeholder Classification (examples follow)
    a. Biz Partner
    b. Board of Directors Member
    c. Contractors / Temp
    d. Customer
    e. Employee Owner
    f. Employee (non-vested)
    g. Stockholder (retired / separated)
    h. Trustee
    i. Vendor
    j. Other (please define below):

3. Date of Conversation

4. Conversation Format
    a. Face to Face
    b. Phone
    c. Video Conference
    d. Other (please define)

5. Stakeholder Feedback (what we heard from Stakeholders)

Leadership is seeing the oak tree in the acorn.
Maria Cortez

Prioritization Worksheet

<u>Step 1</u>: List your **top 10** Core Values, Beliefs, Behaviors, Stakeholder Needs or whatever you are prioritizing (don't worry about putting them in a priority order yet)

a. _____   f. _____

b. _____   g. _____

c. _____   h. _____

d. _____   i. _____

e. _____   j. _____

<u>Step 2</u>: Compare each in groups of two, circle the highest priority in each of the two match-ups below:

a	a	a	a	a	a	a	a	a
b	c	d	e	f	g	h	i	j

b	b	b	b	b	b	b	b
c	d	e	f	g	h	i	j

c	c	c	c	c	c	c
d	e	f	g	h	i	j

d	d	d	d	d	d
e	f	g	h	i	j

e	e	e	e	e
f	g	h	i	j

f	f	f	f
g	h	i	j

g	g	g
h	i	j

h	h
i	j

i
j

My Top 5

1. _____

2. _____

3. _____

4. _____

5. _____

You may create a Wordle at:
http://www.wordle.net/create
Note: must use a browser that supports JAVA
(Chrome does not support JAVA)

Count up # of "wins" for each:

a____   b____   c____   d____   e____   f____   g____   h____   i____   j____

The top by vote are (insert letters here, circle the priorities at the top of the page, add to **My Top 5**:

#1 _____   #2 _____   #3 _____   #4 _____   #5 _____

Adapted from Appendix E, "Where Do I Go With My Life?" by Crystal & Bolles

Prioritization Worksheet

<u>Step 1:</u>   List your **top 10** Core Values, Beliefs, Behaviors, Stakeholder Needs or whatever you are
prioritizing (don't worry about putting them in a priority order yet)

a. _____   f. _____

b. _____   g. _____

c. _____   h. _____

d. _____   i. _____

e. _____   j. _____

<u>Step 2:</u> Compare each in groups of two, circle the highest priority in each of the two match-ups below:

a	a	a	a	a	a	a	a	a
b	c	d	e	f	g	h	i	j

b	b	b	b	b	b	b	b
c	d	e	f	g	h	i	j

c	c	c	c	c	c	c
d	e	f	g	h	i	j

d	d	d	d	d	d
e	f	g	h	i	j

e	e	e	e	e
f	g	h	i	j

f	f	f	f
g	h	i	j

g	g	g
h	i	j

h	h
i	j

i
j

My Top 5

1. _____

2. _____

3. _____

4. _____

5. _____

You may create a Wordle at:
http://www.wordle.net/create
Note: must use a browser that supports JAVA
(Chrome does not support JAVA)

Count up # of "wins" for each:

a____   b____   c____   d____   e____   f____   g____   h____   i____   j____

The top by vote are (insert letters here, circle the priorities at the top of the page, add to **My Top 5**:

#1 _____   #2 _____   #3 _____   #4 _____   #5 _____

Adapted from Appendix E. "Where Do I Go With My Life?" by Crystal & Bolles

S.M.A.R.T Goals

This page is intended to give you insight to the value of goals, the critical elements of S.M.A.R.T goals and general guidance to building effective goals that are both valid and inspiring.

Good goals inspire us and give us purpose[1]. Good goals provide focus and provide the team with fuel for energetic behaviors. Bad goals come across as fraudulent and drain the organization of trust and vitality. Leaders must ensure they use valid S.M.A.R.T goals, and when the team develops goals, these also need to be S.M.A.R.T.

S.M.A.R.T goals come in various forms. The table below illustrates common variations of the concept (items in **bold** are further defined in the Suggested Guidelines in the lower table):

1	**S**	**Specific**	**Simple**	Straight-forward	Shared
2	**M**	**Measurable**	Motivational	Meaningful	Mindful
3	**A**	**Achievable**	Actionable	Attainable	Accountable
4	**R**	**Relevant**	Results-Oriented	Realistic	Repeatable
5	**T**	**Time-Bound**	Time-Targeted	Thorough	Tested

The following are a few guidelines around developing S.M.A.R.T goals. This is not an exhaustive list:

#	S.M.A.R.T Goals - Suggested Guidelines
1	**Specific & Simple:** It is clear what the goal will accomplish. The team understands how and why it will be accomplished. Team members easily and accurately describe the goal and can put it into their own words. Specific and Simple allow people to relate to and align with the goal. Lofty are not really goals at all, and they should be referred to as a vision or conceptual framework (goal clarity is important for building trust) *Fraudulent goals:* Goals that at first seem inspiring, but upon examination are challenging to understand or explain to others. Vague and complex goals leave us with a feeling of feebleness and make it hard to figure out how we participate (contributing to a lack of value in ourselves, our purpose and the goal).
2	**Measurable:** It can be clear, from an empirical (numerical or yes/no) standpoint whether the goal has been, or has not been reached. Measurable goals allow us to be accountable for success and help us hold others to a standard we can commonly understand. Measurable is the most critical aspect of good S.M.A.R.T goals. *Fraudulent goals:* Goals that leave us wondering because no-one understands how to win (or lose). These types of goals undermine the entire organization and focus energy on wondering 'what?' vs figuring out how to win.
3	**Achievable**: Good goals 'feel' possible and raise positive emotional responses. If others have achieved it, it seems more real. If the goal is a stretch, consider mentioning the knowledge, abilities, tools and resources available to help the team be successful. Achievable goals are inspiring and help us want to work hard and learn. *Fraudulent goals:* Goals so lofty they are unattainable defeat us and drain the very life of desire from the team. The focus quickly goes to defense and protection instead of victory.
4	**Relevant:** Goals must be relevant to the Higher Purpose of the organization and directly add value to the Stakeholder community. Relevant goals add to the energy of our purpose and inspire the team to put forth the effort needed to serve Stakeholders. *Fraudulent goals:* Goals that leave us wondering as to their value begin to drain leadership and the organization of trust. If goals do not add value to our Higher Purpose, then 'what and whom are we working for ?' Teams no longer need or want to make the boss successful, they want the organization's Stakeholders to feel successful.
5	**Time-Bound:** Good goals have a clear beginning and end (dates). Any goal over 90 days should be parsed into shorter time-frames (most people cannot imagine beyond 90 days). Clear time-frames give us an understanding of the boundaries and help us focus energy to get the goal accomplished. *Fraudulent goals:* Goals without a time-frame are boundless ideologies that are hard to act upon. We don't know how hard to push or how fast to run. Lack of time-frame leaves us rudderless.

---

[1] In the research report, *The Craving Mind*, Yale University Press, 2017, the authors found that people with no goals had similar brain scans to people who where clinically depressed. ISBN-13: 978-0300223248

S.M.A.R.T Goals - Exercise

This exercise is meant to give you practice at evaluating goals and setting good/better ones.

Look at each goal below. Determine if it is a good S.M.A.R.T goal and if not, re-write it into a good S.M.A.R.T goal. If it's a good goal, could it be improved?

1. A coach announces at the beginning of a season, "We will score more points than ever before."

   As inspirational as this might sound, it's a terrible goal, there is no specificity, there is no measure, we don't know if its achievable, it could be relevant, and there is no time-frame. A good S.M.A.R.T goal might be: I expect this team to increase our point average by 10% (specific, measurable and probably achievable) by the middle of the season (time-bound). On average, we lost games last year by a 7% margin, so 10% puts us in the winner's circle (relevant). I expect every player to be a team player and help others to win. There is no star in team, we practice together, play together, learn together, win together and lose together. We walk on and off the field as a team. Only as a team.

2. The VP of Operations declares, "Over the next 3 months, this team will reduce backorders by 50%. The pilot proved we can do it and I believe in every one of you!"

   _____

   _____

   _____

3. The manager states at a meeting, "This team is capable of delivering 100% quality."

   _____

   _____

   _____

4. Based on your discussions with Stakeholders , write a S.M.A.R.T goal for yourself or for your team:

   _____

   _____

S	**Specific**	**Simple**	Straight-forward	Shared
M	**Measurable**	Motivational	Meaningful	Mindful
A	**Achievable**	Actionable	Attainable	Accountable
R	**Relevant**	Results-Oriented	Realistic	Repeatable
T	**Time-Bound**	Time-Targeted	Thorough	Tested

"Everything should be made as simple as possible, but no simpler."   Albert Einstein

These pages are for exploring, discussing and thinking deeply about Everyday Practical Leadership and real-world application of the model in your world.

Remember, your end game is:

Attract, Inspire and Retain the right Stakeholders!

On each of the next 6 pages, write and explore:

1. Where I can use the model and this tenet *(ideas for implementation, be specific, not too broad)*
2. Benefits[1] of using this EPL tenet with my team *(problems I need to solve or opportunities I need to create)*
3. Disadvantages and challenges of using this EPL tenet with my team *(where I might run into challenges/culture[2] issues)*
4. Ideas for implementation of this tenet *(how do I get started on each one of the tenets)*
5. Creating a Timeline for Success *(action plan)*

The summary of Everyday Practical Leadership is below for reference.

Tenets	Summary of each Tenet
1. Building Enthusiasm	To be inspired or engaged in my work, I have to care about it. This tenet takes you and your team through a safe and motivating process of figuring out your YES; why you care about each other and what you do. Skip this tenet and what your organization does (your YES), for 67% [2] of your employees is just work.
2. Conditions for Victory (CFV)	Everyone must know, empirically what it means to win, or they really don't know how to fully participate or if what they do matters. This tenet gives the power of winning at elements that serve your YES, discovered above, over to your team. Skip this tenet and you will forever be the one coming up with answers (vs. your team inspired to create a better future).
3. Achieving Results	All teams want to know the score. This tenet puts scoring in the hands of the team and helps them to know they are winning. Skip this tenet and you lose A players that want to win, B players that want to learn and you keep C players that you don't want (it becomes a race to the bottom for talent).
4. Enabling Success	The tools and training to do the job are required to win. This tenet takes a unique look at this often 'assumed' process. Skip this tenet and your team is powerless to deliver results.
5. Developing Wisdom	Sharing our learning as a team helps us grow. This tenet supports team growth and learning by use of a safe 'Continuous Improvement' process. Skip this tenet and your will repeat mistakes, never build (or rebuild) a sense of 'team' and be caught in a cycle of slow regression to failure.

[1] **Benefits** – people talk about difference between a 'feature, advantage, benefit.' It's very simple if you look at it this way:

- **Feature** – a distinctive attribute or aspect of something, such as 'my team produces 500 widgets a day.'
- **Advantage** - a condition or circumstance that puts one in a favorable or superior position, such as 'my team produces widgets for 25% less than our competition.'
- **Benefit** – Something that solves a problem or creates an opportunity for your Stakeholder community, such as 'our widgets enable our Stakeholders to lead a healthy lifestyle for less cost than our competitor.' Look at the benefits of using Everyday Practical Leadership in the light of solving a problem or creating an opportunity for your team.

[2] **Culture** – this comes from repetitive behavior. If something worked once, we repeat it, if we do it again and it works, we keep repeating. This creates culture.

Tenet #1 - Building Enthusiasm

You cannot shake hands with a clenched fist. *Indira Gandhi*

1. Building Enthusiasm	
❖ Role Models	1. Agree we are a team and we represent ourselves and each other all the time
❖ Know Core Stakeholders	2. Map Core Stakeholders as a team (the ones we focus on)
❖ Stakeholder Needs	3. Team members meet with Stakeholders and report on Stakeholder Needs[1]
❖ Higher Purpose	4. Produce a set of Team Core Values[2] – what we commit to, what we stand for
❖ Shared Core Values	5. Generate a team set of 'Beliefs & Behaviors' to support Core Values
	6. Create Team Vision Board – where we are going, values, beliefs, behaviors
	7. Develop Team Higher Purpose based on Stakeholder Needs and Core Values

1. Where I can use the model and this tenet *(ideas for implementation, be specific, not too broad)*
2. Benefits[1] of using this EPL tenet with my team *(problems I need to solve or opportunities I need to create)*
3. Disadvantages and challenges of using this EPL tenet with my team *(where I might run into challenges/culture[2] issues)*
4. Ideas for implementation of this tenet *(how do I get started on each one of the tenets)*

_____

_____

_____

_____

_____

_____

_____

_____

_____

_____

_____

_____

_____

The most powerful weapon on earth is the human soul on fire.

MARSHALL FERDINAND FOCH

Tenet #2 - Defining the Conditions for Victory

If you cannot do great things, do small things in a great way. Napoleon Hill

2. Conditions for Victory (CFV)	1. Team creates a S.M.A.R.T. Goal based on Stakeholder Needs honoring Higher Purpose, Core Values and Beliefs
❖ Team Built Goals	2. Goal time should be 2 – 4 weeks out, no longer
❖ Stakeholder & Higher Purpose Focused	3. Set the date for #5 – Developing Wisdom (and how you will celebrate)
❖ S.M.A.R.T. Goals	4. Goal must have everyone involved – no one person/few can carry the team
	• S.M.A.R.T. - *Simple	Measurable	Attainable	Realistic	Time-Bound (see Appendix 4 for more details)*

1. Where I can use the model and this tenet *(ideas for implementation, be specific, not too broad)*
2. Benefits[1] of using this EPL tenet with my team *(problems I need to solve or opportunities I need to create)*
3. Disadvantages and challenges of using this EPL tenet with my team *(where I might run into challenges/culture[2] issues)*
4. Ideas for implementation of this tenet *(how do I get started on each one of the tenets)*

_____

_____

_____

_____

_____

_____

_____

_____

_____

_____

_____

_____

_____

_____

_____

_____

_____

> Where there is unity there is always victory.
> – Publilius Syrus

Coming together is a beginning; keeping together is progress; working together is success.   Henry Ford

3. Achieving Results	1. Team determines how to score the Conditions for Victory and team members do the scorekeeping (not the leader)
❖ Team Developed Scoring & Updating	2. Tracking must be visual and public on how each team member and the team are tracking toward CFV
❖ Visual and Public	3. Only the team wins, no person or group carries the team
❖ Only Team Can Win	

1. Where I can use the model and this tenet *(ideas for implementation, be specific, not too broad)*
2. Benefits[1] of using this EPL tenet with my team *(problems I need to solve or opportunities I need to create)*
3. Disadvantages and challenges of using this EPL tenet with my team *(where I might run into challenges/culture[2] issues)*
4. Ideas for implementation of this tenet *(how do I get started on each one of the tenets)*

_____

_____

_____

_____

_____

_____

_____

_____

_____

_____

_____

_____

_____

_____

_____

_____

_____

Tell me and I forget. Teach me and I remember. Involve me and I learn. Benjamin Franklin

4. Enabling Success	
❖ Supportive Practices & Policies ❖ Actionable Tools ❖ Education	1. Leader must ensure that organizational practices, policy, and procedures are supportive of the Conditions for Victory 2. The Team requests tools and education necessary to meet the CFV 3. Leader searches for tools and education to enable victory – ask the questions, 'What do we need for victory? What is in our way?' 4. Training comes from inside expertise as often as possible 5. Remind team of the date for #5 – Developing Wisdom

1. Where I can use the model and this tenet *(ideas for implementation, be specific, not too broad)*
2. Benefits[1] of using this EPL tenet with my team *(problems I need to solve or opportunities I need to create)*
3. Disadvantages and challenges of using this EPL tenet with my team *(where I might run into challenges/culture[2] issues)*
4. Ideas for implementation of this tenet *(how do I get started on each one of the tenets)*

If you are not willing to learn, no one can help you. If you are determined to learn, no one can stop you.

Tenet # 5 - Developing Wisdom

Learning never exhausts the mind. *Leonardo da Vinci*

5. Developing Wisdom	
❖ **Review** ❖ **Celebration** ❖ **Learning**	1. Before the session, remind team members to bring thoughts around R/W/D/H or C/S/S/H to the session in writing. 2. Invite Stakeholders to be involved in these sessions whenever possible 3. Use the Parking Lot with Post-Its during the session (stay on target) 4. Run the review session using R/W/D/H (Right/Wrong/Different/How) or C/S/S/H (Continue/Stop/Start/How[3]) 5. Celebration only occurs when the team goal(s) is achieved – we honor effort and celebrate success

1. Where I can use the model and this tenet *(ideas for implementation, be specific, not too broad)*
2. Benefits[1] of using this EPL tenet with my team *(problems I need to solve or opportunities I need to create)*
3. Disadvantages and challenges of using this EPL tenet with my team *(where I might run into challenges/culture[2] issues)*
4. Ideas for implementation of this tenet *(how do I get started on each one of the tenets)*

Organizations learn only through individuals who learn. Individual learning does not guarantee organizational learning. But without it no organizational learning occurs.

Peter Senge

- **Gallup State of the American Workplace study, 2017** - http://news.gallup.com/reports/199961/state-american-workplace-report-2017.aspx
- **The Craving Mind:** From Cigarettes to Smartphones to Love – Why We Get Hooked and How We Can Break Bad Habits, **Publisher:** Yale University Press, **ISBN-13:** 978-0300234367
- Quotes from: https://www.brainyquote.com/quotes/lou_holtz_629648?src=t_rules
- **Reinventing Organizations** by Frederic Laloux, ISBN-13: 978-2960133509
- **Transitions: Making Sense of Life's Changes,** published by Da Capo Lifelong Books, written by Dr. William Bridges, ISBN-13: 978-0738209043
- **The Art Of Powerful Questions**, by Eric E.Vogt, Juanita Brown, and David Isaacs; ISBN 0-9724716-1-8, published by Whole Systems Associates

About the Authors

Robert Freese

Bob has been facilitating leadership, change management and organizational development experiences for over 20 years. Currently, he spends most of his time facilitating the transformational leadership experience at the MCC Corporate College in upstate NY.

When not teaching, Bob is either exploring the world with Peggy or working on his romance and fantasy trilogy – Journey, the love story of the century. Bob's pen name is Catlan Samuels.

Bill Gooding

Bill Gooding is a retired leader. Bill developed the Everyday Practical Leadership (EPL) model as he endeavored to help his teams tackle some of the more wicked problems in industry. Through strategic thinking, doing the right thing, constantly learning and relentless patience, Bill's approach solidified over the years.

Bill has used the EPL model with his teams to enable success for over 30 years. Through refinement and feedback, the system has taken on its current form.

Bill is retired now and wanders the hills and forests of Kentucky. We wish him nothing but peace!

To our readers and practitioners
We wish you nothing but success - go ahead, change the world, that is what leaders do!

Made in the USA
Middletown, DE
20 September 2024

61059989R00035